Gianluigi Nuzzi and **Claudio Antonelli**
are acclaimed journalists in their native Italy, where
Blood Ties (originally published as *Metastasi*) was
a No.1 bestseller. Nuzzi is the author of a
previous bestseller, *Vatican Spa.*

BLOOD TIES

THE 'NDRANGHETA: ITALY'S NEW MAFIA

....

Gianluigi Nuzzi and Claudio Antonelli

Adapted from a translation by Jonathan Hunt

PAN BOOKS

First published 2012 by Pan Books
an imprint of Pan Macmillan, a division of Macmillan Publishers Limited
Pan Macmillan, 20 New Wharf Road, London N1 9RR
Basingstoke and Oxford
Associated companies throughout the world
www.panmacmillan.com

ISBN 978-1-4472-0562-3

Copyright © Gianluigi Nuzzi and Claudio Antonelli 2010
Translation copyright © Jonathan Hunt 2012

Originally published in Italian as *Metastasi* 2010 by Chiaralettere, Milan

The right of Gianluigi Nuzzi and Claudio Antonelli to be identified as the
authors of this work has been asserted by them in accordance
with the Copyright, Designs and Patents Act 1988.

The right of Jonathan Hunt to be identified as the
translator of this work has been asserted by him in accordance
with the Copyright, Designs and Patents Act 1988.

1 3 5 7 9 8 6 4 2

A CIP catalogue record for this book is available from the British Library.

Printed and bound by CPI Group (UK) Ltd, Croydon, CR0 4YY

Visit www.panmacmillan.com to read more about all our books
and to buy them. You will also find features, author interviews and
news of any author events, and you can sign up for e-newsletters
so that you're always first to hear about our new releases.

Contents

....

Foreword

· ·

The first copy of this book was presented, together with a written account of its contents, to the public prosecutor Giancarlo Capaldo, the director of the District Anti-mafia Office in Rome. It was our duty to give the magistrates advance notice of any matters of judicial significance that might be relevant to their investigations. Various passages in the book identify the instigators and the direct perpetrators of hitherto unsolved or even unknown crimes.

It goes without saying that all our informants' statements and any accusations that may be contained in them are subject to verification by the magistrates. Any people mentioned in connection with criminal activity must be considered innocent until the judicial authorities have carried out a thorough investigation.

PROLOGUE

....

The opportunity came out of the blue during the winter of 2009 and it had to be seized at once, or the story would have vanished back into the darkness whence it came. I was sitting at my desk in the newspaper office in the late afternoon when the phone rang. It was the newsroom assistant: 'I'm putting a man through to you. It's an unusual case.' If the call had got through the first filter, it must be important. I heard the connection click through to my phone and, at once, the southern accent: 'Hello. I'm a state witness.' There was an intake of breath, then a pause. The voice was quiet and conveyed no emotion, no tone. It went on: 'I want to tell my story.'

This book is based on the exclusive confessions of Giuseppe Di Bella, who left the 'Ndrangheta – something few members of the organization have ever done – after half a century of total loyalty. He had taken the irrevocable decision to turn state's evidence. Di Bella was a boyhood

....

friend, and for many years a trusted associate, of Franco Coco Trovato, one of the organization's bosses, a Calabrian godfather who used violence to establish control over a vast swathe of northern Italy, from Lombardy to the Veneto. His testimony makes it clear how the 'Ndrangheta has successfully penetrated Italian politics, local government, the labour market and businesses large and small, poisoning the population and penetrating even into Parliament, spreading like a cancer throughout the nation.

As an insider, Di Bella knows the 'Ndrangheta's codes, its unwritten laws and its rituals; he describes its first steps into arms trafficking, acquiring weapons from former Second-World-War partisans, its ability to buy anyone and everything, swallowing up companies, shops, lawyers, accountants, and – quite simply – people's whole lives.

Giuseppe Di Bella's credibility is based on several factors. He has always been regarded as a reliable witness by the magistrates and courts that have heard his testimony, in Varese, Como, Milan, Bergamo and other northern Italian towns. Thanks to him, dozens of members of the 'Ndrangheta have been arrested and convicted. This reputation for reliability undoubtedly speaks in his favour, though of course it does not in itself constitute sufficient corroboration of his statements. State witnesses are not oracles or repositories of revealed truth, and every declaration made by Di Bella, however plausible, must be viewed with due scepticism. But three crucial points should be borne in mind.

Firstly, in this book Di Bella reveals his own direct involvement in a series of major crimes, crimes which, until now, were unknown to the anti-mafia investigators. By so doing he is running the risk of incurring new charges and of jeopardizing his relationship with the authorities. Self-accusation lends credibility to any prospective state witness, and Di Bella has been one for a decade.

Secondly, with regard to the most important episodes, Di Bella is not retailing hearsay evidence, but reporting on events in which he himself participated. He himself saw and heard the most dramatic events. Moreover, much of what he says is corroborated by the testimony of another important state witness, Filippo Barreca. The two men have never met – Barreca's criminal activities took place in an area 1200 kilometres away from Di Bella's and never overlapped with them – and yet their stories interlock and complement each other.

Thirdly, since Di Bella is no longer under police protection, and has not been for several months now, and since he has accused members of the 'Ndrangheta of new crimes, he is exposing himself to grave danger, even though he refuses to go back under cover.

But why are these former 'men of honour' speaking out only now? Or, to put it another way, why have they only now decided to make important new information public, in addition to the testimony that they have already given to the magistrates? Barreca, at least, is only corroborating a few specific episodes, but Di Bella is at the end of a long personal journey, which has led him to the point where he has chosen to ignore his lawyer's advice.

'Three or four years ago I told my lawyer that I wanted to make some new statements, but my lawyer said, "No, keep what you know to yourself; don't say anything else." So I followed his advice, but I promised myself that one day I'd say all the things I was dissuaded from saying at the time.

'Then my wife died. As she lay dying I promised her I'd come clean about everything, in order to give our son a future. She was a good person, and over time she altered the course of my life. She tried to change me and she succeeded. She was the reason I turned state's evidence, and when she died I finally understood that there is no friendship in the mafia, only self-interest and death. It's unequivocal. If you don't do what they say, you're finished. Once, before a meeting between some members of the 'Ndrangheta and of Cosa Nostra, including Giovanni Brusca, who detonated the bomb that blew up Giovanni

Falcone, a boss said to me, "The princes and barons are untouchable, because they pull the strings of the political puppets. They control politics." But that's not going to stop me. I'm not frightened any more. I've decided to tell the whole story and lead you into this hell.'

Di Bella's original witness statements – perhaps his most important – were crucial to the investigation into, and subsequent conviction of, his old friend Franco Coco Trovato. They date from the period 2002–5, when he reported in particular 'on the criminal structure of the association and on the evolution of the activities of the "Trovato family"'. So reads the text of the verdict of the Milanese Court of Appeal in 2009, presided over by Cesare Beretta, in a case against the clan to which Di Bella belonged, and which his statements and confessions broke up. More especially, 'Di Bella made a number of statements in twenty-nine interviews in the period from October 2002 to March 2005 . . . This was deemed to be an attenuating circumstance, in view of the importance of his contribution to preventing criminal activity from leading to further consequences.' His contribution consisted of making lengthy witness statements and providing information crucial to the identification of the perpetrators of the various crimes. For this reason, 'considering the significance of the contribution made by Di Bella in relation to the crime of mafia-style criminal association, the maximum reduction' of the sentence (to a period of two years four months) 'appears justified'. After his release and, more importantly, after Trovato's incarceration, Di Bella went underground. No one knew where he was. But you could be sure the organization was trying to find him.

1

THE FIRST MEETING

'I come from the south and I've made a decision.' The voice is steady, with only the slightest hint of nervousness. He doesn't sound like a lunatic; he is talking off the cuff, not delivering a prepared speech. He is wary, but there is no pose about him. I adopt a measured tone, trying to say something to reassure him and open up a dialogue so that I can rule out the possibility that he's a crank. I try to form a link and show him that I can be trusted, but he doesn't seem to be listening.

'I'm from Calabria. I'm under police protection.'

An 'Ndrangheta member who has turned state's evidence, then – one of the few to violate the blood pact between the clan and the family, to reveal the secrets of the ruthless criminal and military organization that is over-taking Cosa Nostra, the mafia of the godfathers and whose turnover is now comparable to that of Microsoft. But what was his rank in the organization?

I hazard a question: 'What's your name?'

Another pause. 'No no, I'm not telling you that over the phone, are you kidding? You can call me Angelo, but you can take it from me it's a false name. Are you interested in my story? If you're not, I'll say goodbye.'

I play for time: 'Yes, I certainly am interested. Listen, I'd like to know how long you've been a state witness.'

'Ten years, but I don't want to keep these things to myself any more. My lawyer advised me not to tell the magistrates anything more, to stop talking. I've filled out reams of preliminary statements and now I'm alone with my memories, my grief and nothing else. "Keep those stories to yourself," the lawyer said. "The authorities don't need any more evidence." I was afraid. I didn't understand and I thought that if I revealed everything I'd be killed, leaving my wife and my son alone. But now I'm not scared any more.'

The words that come down the phone line are as cold as ice.

'Tell me, who was your boss?'

'My phone card has nearly run out . . .'

So I test him: 'Let's meet.'

His reaction is instant and brusque: 'How much is your word, your head, worth?'

I don't understand. 'Take it easy, Angelo. Let's meet and talk face to face,' I reassure him. I feel a bit stupid, trying to assess the words of this state witness, struggling to gain his confidence. I don't even know who he is – a phoney or a real state witness. And yet, as the seconds pass, I have a feeling that this unknown voice is worth checking out.

'The day after tomorrow, at nine.' He mentions the name of a bar, and before I have time to reply, he hangs up.

It's a very risky meeting. I need some help. I discuss the matter with my colleague Claudio Antonelli. I ask him to join me on this assignment. He was a *carabiniere* before he became a journalist and has a keen interest in legal matters. We decide to go together.

At eight o'clock we're already there. We park some distance away so that no one can note down our numberplate. The location is the centre of a small town, indistinguishable from many others in Emilia. Restaurants, cafés, shops. The place chosen for the meeting is a bar-cum-patisserie. It has an L-shaped counter; there is a queue for cappuccinos and croissants, and two female bartenders wearing ghastly caps. It's a strange place for a private meeting. Too crowded, too noisy; very few tables – four in all – and they're visible from outside. Very exposed. We feel disappointed, and rather uneasy.

Not wanting to hang around for too long, we go out to buy a newspaper and come back a few minutes before nine. Some old ladies are sitting at the tables. Claudio stays outside and goes into the shop opposite the bar. I cross the road and enter. 'A coffee, please.' The minutes pass. There's no sign of him. Either he's late or he's not coming. I turn round, go out of the bar, walk thirty metres away and look at the sign, searching for some detail that we might have missed: but no, this is the right bar. I go back inside. I see the tables, the coffee machine and, behind it, a handrail and some stairs I hadn't noticed before. I point to them casually.

'They lead to our afternoon tea room, on the first floor.'

What an amateur. I smile and walk upstairs.

The steps lead into gloom: muffled silence, dim lighting, closed windows, about fifteen tables in all. A man is sitting at the table in the middle of the room, staring at me. At the next table, sideways on, sits a little boy, gazing into the void. He must be about nine or ten. It's like a stage set. What's that kid doing here, in an 'Ndrangheta case, I wonder. An unexpected presence, and a disconcerting one.

'He's my son. I didn't know who to leave him with. I've just moved house; I haven't found him a school yet.' The man anticipates my question, with an apologetic expression.

'Hi! How are you?' I say to the boy. He doesn't react. There's tension, bemusement and despair in his eyes; in his stiff, unmoving posture, in the patches of eczema that cover his arms and disfigure his neck. His father raises his eyes to the ceiling for an interminable moment. There is darkness mingled with loneliness in those eyes. I sit down and we talk. We sit there for several hours. Angelo is cagey and suspicious, but he makes one small concession. He understands my uneasiness and agrees to let Claudio come upstairs.

The boy sits there all the time with his back to us. He doesn't turn round, doesn't speak, doesn't drink, doesn't ask for anything. Only later will we learn that he is eleven years old and is there in that bar with his father – whose name is Giuseppe, not Angelo: Giuseppe 'Pippo' Di Bella – because his mother died of cancer after a six-month illness.

Pippo Di Bella was born in 1951 at Caronia, in the province of Messina, Sicily, but later moved to the province of Lecco, in Lombardy, with his family. He worked for a quarter of a century in the direct employ of the boss Franco Coco Trovato, who in the 1980s became one of the leaders of the 'Ndrangheta in northern Italy. In Lombardy he was the head of a cartel of families which controlled entire provinces – from Milan to Lecco, Como and Varese – and were allied with powerful clans in other regions.

Now Coco Trovato is in prison, but his organization is not defunct – far from it. The business is run by his sons and his brother.

2

UP NORTH

Peace reigns in northern Italy. But only on the surface. The private universities are full of the third-generation scions of the old godfathers; the billion-dollar cake of Expo 2015 – the World Fair, which is to be hosted by Milan – is ready to be sliced up, and the business community is defenceless. You only have to listen to the alarm sounded by Claudio De Albertis, the chairman of Assimpredil, the builders' association representing the provinces of Milan, Lodi, Monza and Brianza: 'They impose restrictions on us in the building sites; the authorities are supposed to be helping us, but all they do is hold back our work without giving us any real protection. We can't act as "building-site policemen" ourselves. We're helpless in the face of the 'Ndrangheta. Before a new contract is signed, the authorities don't provide us with the tools and information we need to defend ourselves and keep out the clans with their honest-looking faces. We're hostages to our own fear, to the cancer that's spreading through the property world. Nobody talks about it, but that's what it's like – a devastating cancer.'

It's only discussed in very restricted circles, but even in Milan the peace ended in November 2009, when a former state witness, Lea Garofalo, was kidnapped, murdered and dissolved in fifty litres of acid. *Lupara bianca*, they call it: 'white shotgun' – seizing someone, killing them and obliterating their bodies. It was the first case of its kind in Milan. For the city the shock gave way to the shame of having to admit that even here the 'Ndrangheta is far from being defeated; on the contrary, it's flourishing. The story of Lea Garofalo, who originally came from Calabria, takes us back in time: in a city of fashion, design, radical chic and avant-garde architecture, it lifts the lid on cruelties we thought were perpetrated only by Cosa Nostra. Like the tragedy of Giuseppe di Matteo, the thirteen-year-old boy who was dissolved in acid in 1996 in Sicily. His father, Santino, was testifying against the bosses behind the assassination of Capaci. The Corleone mafia clan eliminated his son.

Some people think the 'Ndrangheta may send out even

bloodier signals after the outburst of intimidatory violence with which it has unsuccessfully been trying to send messages to the authorities since the beginning of the year: from the gas cylinder that blew up outside the Public Prosecutor's office in Reggio Calabria, to the car packed with weapons and explosives that was found at Reggio airport on the day when the President of the Republic, Giorgio Napolitano, was due to pay an official visit to the city, to the envelopes containing bullets that were sent to the magistrates engaged in the fight against the *'ndrine* ('Ndrangheta clans), and the M80 'Zolja' rocket-launcher found 300 metres away from the Anti-mafia Office in Reggio Calabria in October 2010. The most radical decision, the outcome of which is unpredictable, would be to shift the theatre of confrontation from Calabria to the north, thus raising the level of perception of the danger. After all, Calabria has effectively been abandoned by the authorities and is now regarded by many politicians, including some within the government, as a 'lost' region.

The deputy prosecutor of Reggio Calabria, Nicola Gratteri, who is in the front line of major investigations into the 'Ndrangheta, is more cautious: 'The level of the confrontation is likely to stop short of really dramatic gestures, otherwise it would mean that history has taught the 'Ndrangheta nothing. After the mafia war in Calabria, the authorities reacted harshly, with mass trials, and the repercussions for the families were serious. So I think this attack on the institutions in Reggio Calabria should be seen as a limited action at a time when there's a power vacuum. Many bosses have been arrested in various police operations, and new recruits are coming to the fore. These actions may be just trials of strength by people jostling for position to re-establish the internal balance. It's like saying: "I'll plant some bombs and then let's see what happens." I don't think the 'Ndrangheta elite is happy with this strategy. We shouldn't automatically assume that there's an agreement between the godfathers. It's also obvious, and the investigations will show this, that the more violent and intransigent sectors have, by their silence, given their implied assent to the dual interpretation that serious episodes like these demand.'

•

Only one person can explain the link between the past and the future: Filippo Barreca. His revelations were crucial to the struggle against the 'Ndrangheta in the 1990s. They also led to the murder of his brother Vincenzo, who was killed in 2002 in a barber's shop in Reggio Calabria. Barreca was the first 'Ndrangheta state witness to change his identity and even now, eighteen years later, he is living under cover. Having received a lump sum of 1.6 billion lire from the state to assist him in reintegrating into society, today he is a successful businessman and appears as a witness at trials, protected by the ever-present screen which hides his silhouette and his face.

Nicola Gratteri emphasized Barreca's significance in a recent interview that he gave us: 'The *pentiti* ['penitents', i.e. people who have turned state's evidence] phenomenon reached its peak in the 1990s, when there were about two thousand *pentiti* from the Camorra, about one thousand from Cosa Nostra and less than a hundred from the 'Ndrangheta. Moreover, the Calabrian state witnesses were all low-ranking figures and therefore unable to provide an overall view of the situation. Only two of them were important – Franco Pino, the leader of a clan in Cosenza, and Barreca, who was a boss in Pellaro, near Reggio Calabria. None of the real patriarchs of the 'Ndrangheta – I'm thinking of the Nirta-Romeos of San Luca or the Di Stefanos and Condellos of Reggio Calabria – has ever turned state's evidence. We have never had a *pentito* comparable in status to the Sicilian boss Tommaso Buscetta, or even to Giovanni Brusca, who played a key role in the murder of Giovanni Falcone. Nevertheless, Barreca was a *santista*, a member of the *santa*, the highest rank in the so-called *società maggiore*.

Only a member of the *santa* can belong to the freemasons – with whom the 'Ndrangheta have long had links – and thereby have a dual affiliation. Only a member of the *santa* can "sit in the control room", and even be a police informer. The *santa* is a kind of criminal shock-absorber. In order to prevent feuds and murders, a *santista* can decide to report some criminals to the police. The *santa* is a "thermostat" which determines the destinies of many people. To be a member is to be in a very influential position.'

As early as 1979 Barreca had been made a *santista* by the *copiata* – the triad of *capobastone* (local leader), *contabile* (accountant) and *crimine* (literally 'crime', a consultative body which may, as in this case, consist of only one person) – comprising the bosses Santo Araniti, Natale Iamonte and Turi Scriva. So he belonged to the senior, elite level, accessible only to major bosses like Paolo Di Stefano, Antonio Nirta and Mommo Piromalli.

He is the most important of the *pentiti* who are still alive, given the senior role that he held in the organization. We had the opportunity of interviewing him on several occasions, and this is what he told us: 'All my statements were useless – and I made thousands of them. They were useless because I repeated hundreds, thousands of times, to all the magistrates who questioned me on a variety of crimes from Milan to Reggio Calabria, that the 'Ndrangheta is the most powerful organization in the world precisely because there's this family network between its members. The family network enables you to keep your secrets and protect your business dealings. For a long time now the 'Ndrangheta has, in a way, been growing closer to its Sicilian roots. From 1985 onwards, after the second mafia war, with the rise of the a-Tegano-Libri group, they decided to form a commission that followed, and still follows today, the progress of the various families and in particular of their various bars and restaurants. This being the case, it's unthinkable – indeed I would categorically rule out the possibility – that there is no guiding hand behind these latest episodes, these warnings that I've seen on television.'

'It's impossible to carry out such operations without a decree of the *commissione provinciale*, the 'Ndrangheta's local governing committee,' Barreca goes on. 'With regard to these attacks, these threats, there are two possible interpretations of them: they may be intended as more specific ways of applying pressure, of giving warnings, to a certain office of the judiciary, but they definitely also carry a broader, more radical message to the state.'

Barreca does not agree with those who see these 'show' attacks as a manifestation of a limited phenomenon. The 'Ndrangheta has grown now; like Cosa Nostra, it tries to establish a dialogue with the heart of government.

According to Barreca, it cultivates that grey area where legality and illegality blur together, reviving an old approach, a method once adopted by Cosa Nostra in the years of the bomb attacks, after the deaths of the anti-mafia judges Giovanni Falcone and Paolo Borsellino: 'It's not like the 1990s any more. Things have improved, from the 'Ndrangheta's point of view; they've found a way into the political world and the organs of government. As a matter of fact, they've always interacted with the organs of government to a certain extent – and with the political world, and not only in the south, as is shown by the investigations that are currently being made into certain members of the Northern League, the federalist and secessionist north Italian party.

'It all began during the age of kidnappings. Kidnapping had not only an economic but an "institutional" purpose. It was a clear, stark message: "Gentlemen, we can get you any time we want. Anyone can be a target." Certainly, it would have been more profitable for us to sell drugs than to kidnap people, but by kidnapping people we guaranteed that we had some institutional corridors, and those corridors remained open afterwards. In the present circumstances, leaving a car full of explosives in the street on the day of a visit from the President of the Republic means: "Watch out! We're here. If you don't do what we want, we'll strike."

'Obviously I can't be more precise because I'm not in the 'Ndrangheta any more,' Barreca goes on, 'but certainly the objective is easier to identify today: they want a dialogue, that's the nub of it. It doesn't matter what the dialogue is about, or what the reason for it is, but there must be a dialogue: that's very important to the 'Ndrangheta.

'When the car bomb was left for President Napolitano and the threats were made to the magistrates, I said to myself, "This is 1992 all over again." It's certainly possible to make a comparison between what is happening today and the bomb attacks of 1992–3, which had the same aim: that of establishing a dialogue with the authorities so that some sort of compromise could be reached. But the most important point remains the union between the Calabrian 'Ndrangheta and the Sicilian mafia in sending out these signals. Through interlocutors, including members of state organs, it is certainly possible to create the necessary mediation. As in the days of the kidnappings, today force is being used as a basis for negotiation about everything. It's an inevitable development.'

'In my day,' Barreca says in one of our interviews, 'Cosa Nostra had far more power at the political level, without a doubt. Today that's no longer the case. The Calabrian bosses have found a way into the organs of government.

And these recent signals, such as the car bomb, are clear evidence of an "authority" sufficiently powerful to make a dialogue with members of the government possible. As I said before, the 'Ndrangheta has penetrated deep into the social, and even more the political, fabric, by consolidating the economic power that it has gained. My own experience is testimony to this. I used to spend as much as 25,000 euros a day, and sell 600 kilos of cocaine a month, and I was able to escape the police because I always benefited from the mistake that the authorities always make: they underestimate the importance of retaliatory action. That is to say, the means that the authorities deploy today are inferior to the economic and technological power that the 'Ndrangheta possesses.'

There is nothing new in the idea that Italy invests inadequate resources in the fight against organized crime. But what Barreca is saying is different. The 'Ndrangheta has always been thought of as a backward kind of mafia, inexpert at laundering money and lacking the technological awareness typical of other organizations like Cosa Nostra. In fact the reverse is true: for decades the families have been at the cutting edge in their logistical methods, in their use of technology to safeguard the principles that have characterized the 'Ndrangheta from the beginning, such as total secrecy. What Barreca has to say on the subject is very illuminating: 'Even back in the 1980s I already had mobile phones that could tap into a cell of the national network, so that the police couldn't tell where the call was coming from; while the policeman who was tailing me still had to use a call box. And do you know what happened as a result? I sold anti-wire-tapping devices to the San Luca group, which organized the kidnappings in Calabria and helped us in our negotiations with the authorities, something that has never been known until now.'

During that period, technology concealed some disturbing links which, according to Barreca, already involved government offices.

'One episode,' he says, 'will illustrate the strategic importance of the kidnappings, quite apart from the huge amount of money they brought in. One day I had a meeting with Domenico Sica, the high commissioner of the Antimafia Office, near Piazza Cavour in Rome. Sica told me that they were desperate to bring about the liberation of Cesare Casella, the young man who was kidnapped in Pavia in 1988.'

Casella, eighteen years old, the son of a Citroën dealer in Pavia, was the victim of one of the longest and most dramatic kidnappings known in Italy. For two years, until January 1990, he was chained up in the underground caves of Aspromonte, a hostage to protracted negotiations between the 'Ndrangheta and his family. The authorities were caught in the middle, unable to locate the prison or identify the kidnappers.

'Sica was very agitated and wanted a quick solution to the problem: "Pippo," he said to me, "I'm being pressurized on all sides. You've got to get Casella released for me." I looked at him and laughed: "I haven't got Casella in my pocket, you know. I can't just go and fetch him and bring him here to you." He said, "Our secret services are working on it, you know."

'Sica had close connections to the secret services,' Barreca goes on, 'so he knew the spooks had gone into action. And indeed they contacted the kidnappers, through some intermediaries. They paid out a billion and a half, because of course they had access to all the money they needed, and two years later they got Casella released. So the kidnappers, in addition to the ransom they were paid by the family, got a billion and a half lire from the state for releasing him immediately. Public opinion was in a ferment, and the kidnapping was causing political problems. All the money from the ransoms paid for the kidnappings went to the Papalias, in Milan, who reinvested it in drug trafficking and business activities. That was the glue that held the management of the kidnappings together.'

The Casella ransom money enabled the 'Ndrangheta to

build up its capital, giving it the financial clout to enter the business of buying and selling the cocaine of the Colombian cartels.

Casella was set free on the pebble beach of a river at Natile di Careri, a small village between Platì and Bovalino, in the heart of the Locride. More than twenty years have passed since then, but nothing has changed. Careri is just the same now as it was when the Casella boy was kidnapped, as is the whole of Calabria. Cars worth one or two hundred thousand euros drive into the garages of houses with unplastered walls; the dinginess of the streets belies the golden taps in the bathrooms of certain houses.

•

'Once I went to Careri to arrest a boss,' says Deputy Chief of Police Carmine Gallo, who has taken part in investigations into dozens of kidnappings and is regarded as one of the most experienced investigators in the force, 'but the houses there don't have any numbers. I didn't know where he lived. So I asked one of the local traffic police for information. He looked at me blankly and didn't answer. Didn't say a word. I couldn't believe it. I tried to provoke him, to scare him: "I'll arrest you if you don't tell me." My threat had no effect. He didn't give in, even when I clapped the handcuffs on his wrists. I drove him off in my car but he sat in silence for forty kilometres. "If I show you which house it is they'll kill me tonight," he whispered, trembling. I had to go back and get one of his colleagues to point the house out to me, but even he would only do it from a distance.'

It's hard to explain to anyone outside Calabria, let alone a northern Italian, someone from an affluent district like Brianza, say, that there are places where a policeman from out of town has to handcuff a traffic cop just to find out where a criminal lives. When a journalist goes round in the Locride, the 'Ndrangheta will often follow him at a distance. It's a discreet way of tailing someone. In Platì, at the shrine of the Madonna of Polsi, where the bosses meet on 29 September, the feast of St Michael the Archangel, the patron saint of the 'Ndrangheta – who also happens to be the patron saint of the police – they ride along behind you on motor scooters and point blandly up at the sky, as if to say, 'You'd be safer up there, in a plane flying back to Milan.'

Omertà reigns supreme, and an apparent calm prevails everywhere. If you ask the pupils of Careri primary school what the 'Ndrangheta is, they don't know, or at any rate they don't reply. They sit and gaze at you in silence. The head of the local educational authority is the epitome of evasiveness: 'The 'Ndrangheta? There's no 'Ndrangheta in the school. As for what happens outside school, I've no idea; it's not my concern.'

The only kind of crime that gets reported to the local *carabinieri* barracks is the occasional theft of a piece of heavy machinery. 'My wife,' explains Giovanni Capello, who was station commander until August 2010, 'was pregnant and she might as well have been under house arrest. She seldom went out and she lived a life of solitude. They despised us, barely tolerated us. After a while you get used to it, and it doesn't bother you so much. Only today, now that I've been transferred and can look back at the situation from afar, do I understand Careri. I lived there for seven years, and I can hardly believe that I managed to put up with it.'

This small town holds the most dismal record imaginable. It has a higher percentage of men of honour than any other village in the world: six or seven hundred 'Ndrangheta members out of a population of a few thousand, including women and children. Another record was fortunately swept away in a single night, and yet for decades it had been a general source of pride: there had never been a single *pentito* in the whole district: no one had ever been swayed by the national interest, by their conscience or by the number of their relatives that had been killed in feuds. The place simply did not breed informers.

Then in 2006 shame, dishonour and scandal came upon the town. A local man, Rocco Varacalli, born in 1970, kicked over the traces and turned state's evidence, after eighteen years of criminal activity in the Cua-Pipicella clan. 'Rocco has turned *pentito*!' It was a shock. His brother Mimmo and the rest of his family wore black for weeks. They were in mourning, quite literally: Rocco was dead, as far as they were concerned. 'We are no longer his family,' they wrote in a letter to the newspapers. 'He is not, and never has been, worthy to belong to a close-knit, clean-living, honest family like ours. No judgement could ever describe him; we have no words for such a person, and frankly he doesn't deserve any words.'

His family turned away from him – some out of conviction, some because they were scared that they would be killed. It's hard to blame them – they have to live there. That's the way things are in Careri.

So to find a member of the 'Ndrangheta who abandons his comrades, reveals what goes on behind the scenes, breaks all the accepted rules and challenges the organization and his family is very rare. Especially when the person in question is prepared to throw light on the 'Ndrangheta's support network, its infiltration of politics and its links with legitimate business.

3

....

THE INITIATION

We return four more times to that small-town bar after Di Bella leaves the protection programme. Very gradually he comes to trust us, and we establish a relationship. We have dozens of meetings at his home, a flat in a large apartment building where the life of a *pentito* can pass relatively unobserved. There is no name on the entryphone, on the letterbox or by the bell outside his door. He is a ghost. Every time we go there, we sit in his bare kitchen, drinking foul coffee and feeling constantly on edge. The television is always on so that the neighbours can't hear his reminiscences, his stories of blood and money and of respectable citizens who walk arm in arm with the godfathers. The blinds are always rolled down as a precaution. 'Make sure

....

you come dressed as workmen. If a police patrol drops round to check that everything is OK, I'll have the toolbox open where anyone can see it and we'll tell them . . . we'll tell them you're carpenters who've come to fix the front door.' Di Bella prepares everything: a screwdriver and an old lock on the table. If a patrol comes round we'll say we've come to repair it and then go out to buy a new one. But what if the people who knock at the door are not the police?

'If they come here to kill me, obviously they'll kill you too. What do you expect? They're not the mafia, who at least have a little respect for children: the 'Ndrangheta have no respect for children or for anyone. If these people decide to massacre your family, they'll come round and they won't care who they find, whether your cousin is visiting you or anyone else. They'll wipe them all out. You have more chance of reasoning with a mafioso than with an 'Ndranghetista, because an 'Ndranghetista is ignorant, but he takes his orders from intelligent people. There's no point in trying to reason with them, because the bosses say, "OK, we don't want to do this job ourselves, we'll get" – let's say for the sake of argument – "the Romanian to do it. Here's a pistol, Romanian: go round and kill the guy." The Romanian doesn't give a damn whether there might be children present or not. With the mafia it's different: the victim is trussed up like a goat – *incaprettato* – hands and ankles bound together behind their backs; in other words they leave a clear message that it was they who executed him, and they don't send just anyone to do it. Do you see how the system works? That's why the 'Ndrangheta are extremely dangerous: because when they decide to do something they don't care how it's done. They have to get their revenge, that's all that matters to them.

'So it's ninety-nine per cent certain that I'll be killed,' Di Bella goes on, 'but there comes a point where you draw a line, take stock and make an irrevocable decision. Ever since I turned state's evidence I've known that I'm here today but won't be tomorrow. I know the risks I'm taking. I won't die a natural death, I know that; sooner or later they'll get me. But I'm aware of what I'm doing. Yes, it's ninety-nine point nine per cent certain that they'll get me. That's why I'm telling you this. I prefer to get it all off my chest – I'm only a walking ghost now, anyway. The only document I have is my contract with the central protection service; that changes my identity but not my criminal past, about which I've given all the details in twenty-nine interviews with the public prosecutors' offices in Milan, Lecco and Reggio. Twelve hundred euros a month to live without a name and without illusions. I know very well that when someone decides to leave the 'Ndrangheta it can only end one way. Nobody leaves the 'Ndrangheta; the only way anyone leaves the family is feet first. They swear that they'll kill you, and they do.'

But why does he want to talk about those things the lawyer told him to forget about?

'The reason I'm talking today is that my wife, Federica, died. The cancer finished her off in six months, and they wouldn't let me have her treated. The judges wouldn't help me move her to a specialized clinic in Switzerland, to try to save her. It took six months to get an official stamp on the permit to go abroad, and by that time she was dead: the bureaucracy killed her. They didn't even want her parents to come here to say their farewells to her at our home. It was a matter of security, they said; we live in a secret location, and no one must know where it is. But could I deny my wife the chance to say goodbye to her mother and father? No, I let them come, I let them embrace each other. But that's not all. When Federica died, they wouldn't let me follow the coffin at the funeral. I was taken there under escort, and they only let me stay for five minutes after the service. They took me home without allowing me to follow my wife's cortege to her burial. It was dangerous for my security, they said. I had to say my private goodbye to her at the front door of my flat. I live under cover, I don't exist.'

Pippo Di Bella has no regrets about his decision to turn state's evidence, but today he hates himself for having wasted his life fulfilling the criminal dreams of his boss, Franco Coco Trovato, instead of his own. Those dreams have turned into a nightmare: the arrests, the false accusations from accomplices, his decision to become a *pentito*, forced into hiding and, most painful of all, his wife's death from cancer.

•

The story of Di Bella's initiation reads like the screenplay of a film. 'It's all my own fault. When I was young I didn't listen to my father, who was a very honest man. I met Franco – Franco Coco Trovato – the man who brought the 'Ndrangheta to northern Italy, at the parish youth club in Maggianico, a district of Lecco in Lombardy, on the shore of a branch of Lake Como. I was fifteen, maybe sixteen years old. He'd just moved up north from Marcedusa, near Catanzaro, and was already showing leadership potential. As he grew up, he lost interest in scoring goals on the football field or in working as a builder; he preferred stealing other people's money. It was all very minor stuff compared to the later cocaine mules, who were killed by having their stomachs slashed open, the armies of criminals in the 1980s and 1990s and the activities of his heirs in recent years. But you could see what he was like even when he was a boy; he had a criminal nature all of his own. I was immediately impressed by the way he terrorized people and bossed them about – the way he could kill someone just for insulting him.

'But my father didn't approve of him: he saw what he really was and didn't like the way he behaved. So for a while I broke away from Franco, kept my distance. But we were friends and so we soon started doing things together again – "working", in our own way. First it was motor scooters. He was clever: he'd choose his victim, size up his prey, a boy who looked uneasy outside the bar, and then he'd suddenly pull him off the saddle, steal his scooter and threaten him: "You're going to keep quiet, aren't you? What are you going to do about it? Report me to the police? Are you sure you want to do that?"'

These rudimentary methods of intimidation were refined day by day. The gang took shape and diversified its criminal activities.

'We developed progressively: cars, extortion, small-scale cocaine dealing, then robberies. Franco's area of influence began to expand from Olginate, where he was already the boss, to Lecco and Brianza. Wherever he went, he was unstoppable. He took over, and there was no room for anyone else.'

That's how Coco Trovato, aged just nineteen, built his

criminal empire. In twenty years he mustered a following of some 1,400–1,500 people, including all his associates and allies around the world. 'I knew a third of them in person,' says Di Bella. 'If anyone wouldn't cooperate, there was an instant reprisal. A warning, intimidation and then the killing. Franco's character guaranteed him immediate membership of the 'Ndrangheta. They gave him the role of *camorrista*, the second step on the ladder of seniority (the lowest being that of *picciotto*), but by the early 1980s we already knew he was a *santista*, a boss. By the mid-1980s he controlled the whole Lecco area.'

The turning point came in the late summer of 1976. The scene was the Farfallino communist club in Lecco, where the then Italian Communist Party was holding a Festival of Unity. A left-wing activist, Pier Antonio Castelnuovo, forty-two, brother of the actor Nino Castelnuovo, quarrelled with a group of rowdy youths. The newspapers next day reported an animated argument which degenerated into a fight. In fact the unwitting Castelnuovo had come up against Coco Trovato's thugs, who demanded respect from everyone. This was not the suburbs of Reggio Calabria. People weren't used to that kind of thing in Lecco. The upshot was that Castelnuovo was killed. Angelo Musolino was charged but later acquitted of his murder. Musolino was sixteen years old and already destined for a brilliant career in the organization. The fact that he'd killed someone in revenge for an insult was a source of pride, which guaranteed him both a bonus and a successful criminal career. And it was not just Musolino who was rewarded. Coco Trovato gave his young thugs the most sought-after accolade: he immediately had most of them 'baptized' – officially and ritually admitted into the 'Ndrangheta.

'These boys,' Di Bella recalls, 'responded aggressively to Castelnuovo. They said, "What right do you have to come here and order us around?" He said, "Get the hell out of here." Then they started kicking and punching him and just went on and on. Nobody intervened. When someone eventually did step in, it was too late. Castelnuovo was dead. But their vicious behaviour proved their credentials to Coco Trovato. The confrontation had been a test of their courage.'

It is the passing of such tests that makes a baptized man of the 'Ndrangheta feel 'superior' to other men, forging the mentality that drives him to obtain wealth that he would otherwise only dream of, and instils in others a reverential fear which makes him think he is invincible and which would never have been shown to him otherwise.

'With respect to other people,' explains Di Bella, 'a *battezzato* thinks he's a god, and feels like one. He *is* a god. His physique, his build, doesn't matter; once a man enters a criminal organization, even if he is a weakling, from that day on he feels like a god. And if he gets into a quarrel he will do all he can to prove it to the organization: "I'm the best." The *battezzato* no longer regards other people as human beings with a life, a heart, desires and emotions. Other people no longer exist, and if they bother you, you intimidate them or kill them. We members of the 'Ndrangheta don't see other people as people. We ignore them, we think they're all losers, fools, people with no balls who are content to get by on a thousand euros a month, without any dignity, or any pleasure in life.'

It is a perverse system of values, power and supremacy, a machinery of support which makes you regard membership as a social privilege, and the clan as your true family, an elite.

'In the south there's a queue of people outside the boss's door, all hoping to be put to the test so that they can enter the family. But in the north too a lot of people come forward. And once you are in the 'Ndrangheta that can mean only one thing: thinking like the boss, never thinking for yourself, guessing their next move, understanding where there's an opportunity for some business and where that opportunity might end in death. I was always scared, certainly, very scared; I was always scared even of the people who were close to me. Having an 'Ndranghetista, a *camorrista*, close to me, didn't give me any security; I was continually looking over my shoulder, because I never knew how they were going to behave, I never knew what orders they'd received, I never know what they were thinking, especially if they were men of action. It was like having the devil standing next to you; they were liable to kill you, they certainly didn't make you feel stronger. You didn't feel safe even though you knew they were on your side.'

Pippo Di Bella, too, had to prove his worth before being admitted into the criminal organization. He had to carry out every mission that he was given. 'My test was bringing home the family's money. At the age of eighteen I began collecting debts, beating up people who didn't pay, burning cars and warehouses. The assets belonged to people who didn't pay the *pizzo*, the protection money, to Franco. If they didn't pay, we burned their business premises or resorted to strong-arm tactics: beating them up, sending them to hospital, burning their cars, scaring their families. This wasn't Calabria, it was Lombardy. And yet everyone pretended not to see. We were in the clear because all that would happen would be that a short article would appear in the newspaper. The incidents were soon forgotten. Anyone who paid the money was guaranteed: if they suffered a robbery they came to us and it was ninety-nine per cent certain that we would manage to identify who had done it and recover the money. Franco was in contact with the gypsies, the fairground operators, the fences, everyone, the corrupt police and the corrupt *carabinieri*. Even if the *carabinieri* caught them, they pretended not to see them: "Look, Franco, those are the guys who did the robbery. We've let them go, but you know where to find them." The *carabinieri* didn't arrest them, because if they did that our client risked not getting back all the money that had been stolen. That's how the protection racket works, because there are corrupt police out there who get their salary every month from the 'Ndrangheta.'

But as well as collecting the protection money, there were even tougher 'jobs'. Often what lay behind the burning of a warehouse, a furniture store, luxury cars or lorries was not the classic act of extortion: 'We'd intimidate people if their property interested Franco or he wanted to give it to someone else in exchange for a favour. Say they wouldn't give him a warehouse. He'd have it burned down so that he got it on the cheap, taking over the firm. If a bar, or a piece of land, directly interested Franco or some friend, we went into action. If someone said to him, "I'm interested in that house," Franco would reassure him: "There's no problem, I'll see to it, I'll make sure you get it for next to nothing." If a bar interested him and he knew it had a turnover of, say, ten, he would demand fifty as *pizzo*. He'd put the squeeze on them. The owner wouldn't be able to pay, he'd have to sell, and Franco would buy it off him at a bargain price.

'We took one accountant who worked in Valmadrera to the three bridges of Lake Lecco and lowered him head first into the lake from the railway bridge. He was supposed to hand over some buildings he owned, but he had done something wrong, and we were ordered to scare him. We pushed him onto this bridge, tied a rope round his feet, dipped him into the water and lifted him out again until he couldn't take any more and gave in: "All right, all right, I'll sell, I'll do anything you want me to do." And we cleaned him out, poor devil. He had nothing left, we completely ruined him. But there was no choice: either he gave in or we'd have left him to drown there.'

Not coming from an 'Ndrangheta family, Di Bella had to combine his criminal activities with a life that was above suspicion in the eyes of his friends and parents. He had to camouflage himself by learning the art – indispensable to a mafioso – of becoming invisible: 'In those days I had an official job too. Maybe I took a fortnight's sick leave whenever I felt like it, but I had to go to work, as long as my father was alive. Later I set up some bars of my own, but first I worked for six years as a night security guard. That way I found out if this bank or that post office had any money in its vaults, if this or that firm had safes . . . And I'd tell the others, "Hey, boys, there's a safe in this firm, and there could be such-and-such a sum in it."

'We were beginners and we were clumsy. I've never told the magistrates this, but the attack on the Social Security office in Milan in 1986 was the work of the emerging northern 'Ndrangheta. There was only cash in the safe at that time. It was just before Christmas, and I sent some of our boys to the Social Security office; I told them to go to a particular place because I knew there was money there. One morning, before I started my shift, I overheard someone in the boardroom talking about a delicate and important delivery to the Milan branch in Via Melchiorre Gioia, which would have to be made in the evening because the next day they had to make a number of payments. I called a person close to Franco and suggested the robbery. "I can't go tonight," he replied. "I'll send three friends." It made no difference to me. I'd done my duty, by making the phone call. But the three he sent were idiots. They got into the offices and found the safe, but they couldn't open it. So they loaded it into their car. It was an old Fiat, and it nearly collapsed under the weight. They couldn't close the boot, so when they passed a security guard on a bicycle, they took fright and bolted. Two days later I bought a newspaper, *Il Giorno*, and there was a banner headline about the attempted raid on the Social Security office. 300 million lire were found in the abandoned safe. An enormous sum of money, and those fools let it slip through their fingers.'

•

The first rule of the 'Ndrangheta has always been that of blood ties. The organization has a concentric structure in which, roughly speaking, the central part is made up of people linked together by blood ties, a second circle comprises people, not necessarily relatives, who are officially 'baptized', and a third circle consists of people like Di Bella, who are not relatives and are not baptized. The core of this tightly knit structure was blood relationship, and under Franco's regime each member of his immediate family ran a sector of the organization.

Vincenzo Musolino was the financial brains of the organization: he opened estate agencies, waste-disposal companies and restaurants. Vincenzo was the brother of Franco's wife, Eustina, and of Angelo, who had been acquitted of the Castelnuovo murder. Cocaine was the speciality of the brothers Salvatore and Gianni Marinaro, who married Franco's granddaughters. They controlled the trade and had to punish anyone who sold on his own account or who dealt in heroin. 'Heroin is bad for business,' Franco was always saying, and few people dared to contradict him. Anyone who sold heroin got a punishment beating or was even killed.

Blood cements alliances, it strengthens them. The family's big breakthrough was a marriage arranged with a member of the De Stefano family. Franco gave his daughter Giuseppina in marriage to Carmine De Stefano, the favourite son of Paolo De Stefano, one of the Reggio Calabria bosses. When Paolo was killed in the street in 1985, Franco became even more important: he was now the key contact for the Reggio people and the clans in the province of Catanzaro.

'Franco was the last of the bosses,' muses Di Bella. 'Nowadays everything's different. There's no honour in any of the organizations any more. As in the case of Cosa Nostra, the people who have taken the reins of the 'Ndrangheta now are all alike. Honour disappeared when drugs arrived. I've seen people who in the old days you couldn't get to talk even if you put one of their hands on the table and impaled it with a knife. Then I've met those same people ten or fifteen years later after they'd taken to snorting cocaine: you only had to give them a couple of cuffs round the head and they'd tell you all they knew about anyone. It's drugs that have ruined the organization; there's no seriousness any more, there's no reliability, and sometimes I wonder how it will all end. The smart ones will go into politics, into contracts, whereas the ones who deal in drugs and other stuff will fight it out for a share of the market. They'll kill each other – it's inevitable; there's nobody holding them back any more.

'At one time, Franco was still fairly strong, even though he was in prison; he sent messages and orders out. It's possible that he still does today, it's true: if he says that someone needs eliminating they eliminate him. But there isn't the same seriousness there used to be. In the past, every time I sent a message to Franco in prison and it got through, I got what I asked for at once, in the space of a few minutes. Imagine how he'd react now. He must be livid with me: thanks to me, his son Emiliano was sentenced to twenty-two years, and Giacomo Coco Trovato, the son of Mario, Franco's brother, got eighteen or nineteen.'

Maybe because he was born in Sicily, maybe because he never wanted to be tied down, even though Di Bella worked for the gang smuggling drugs and weapons and in white-collar crime he was never formally admitted into the organization; he is not a *battezzato*. He doesn't have the same blood. That may partly explain how he found the courage to inform on them all: 'They wanted me to join the organization formally, but I never would. I'm Sicilian and I didn't want to be baptized by the 'Ndrangheta, a Calabrian organization, because the Sicilians and the Calabrians have always hated each other. If anything had gone wrong, Franco, being the sort of man he was, would have made me pay with my life. That's one of the reasons why I never agreed to it. Another reason was that I was scared of my father. If he'd heard that I'd done something like that he'd have given me another kind of baptism, and done it himself. Family ties are rule number one. And I never completely trusted the family, I mean the Trovato family, which to me *is* the 'Ndrangheta. Because, being a Sicilian, I always felt there was a gap between me and them, that they were on a different rung of the ladder. I didn't think like the boss; I never stopped thinking for myself. I always kept my antennae raised. If you drop your guard for a second, you're gone.

'To understand whether you're in danger of being killed, you have to pay attention to every detail, especially if you disobey an order. For example, if you know you've done something behind Franco's back – maybe you've kept some money back in your own pocket or you've sold arms or drugs on your own account – you have to keep on the alert for weeks. If he reprimands you immediately, that's it: the matter ends there. Franco is going to turn a blind eye to it because you're useful to him and because the amount of money involved isn't significant, and what you've done doesn't represent a threat to his authority. But if he doesn't reprimand you and asks you mysteriously to meet him somewhere, it's time to get worried, to raise your antennae. I never call anyone a fool. I never underestimate even the stupidest person in the world. We have a saying in my village: the cunning man dies at the hand of the idiot.

'Franco Coco Trovato has his own special way of handing down death sentences. If he sends you a message through his right-hand man or his chauffeur, saying, "Meet me in Milan, we need to talk business," you'd better start worrying. If you go to the meeting, they'll kill you. No one who has ever gone to an appointment like that has come home to tell the tale.

'Franco lived a life of business, pleasure and adventure. He certainly didn't have many worries. He drove a different sports car every day – a Ferrari, a Porsche. They threw parties, orgies with lots of women; they brought along enough cocaine for everyone, and they snorted like pigs, it was incredible. I've never seen Franco himself use cocaine, but everyone else in the organization did. I tried it too, of course I did, why should I refuse it? But when I decided that I'd had enough, that was it. But these were people who would put twenty to thirty grams on the plate at a time and snort it, and then go out and commit a crime. They became so mean it was terrifying; hardly surprising in the circumstances. Their heads were clearer than before. Afterwards you wouldn't see them for three or four days because they'd have collapsed and be at home sleeping it off. But unfortunately that was the way it was: everyone I met sniffed cocaine, even Franco's lawyer and accountant friends. Heroin was a different matter, though: anyone who used that was punished.

'This was another thing that strengthened the family ties; and when there was a problem, it was solved. Like the triple murder in Manfredonia, in 1991, when the brothers Pasquale and Michele Pio Placentino and Fabio Tamburrano were killed because they had expanded their field of activity too much.

'But we – the members of his gang – also ran the risk of being killed. Look at Raffaele Laudari. Like Franco, he was born in Catanzaro. They were in the same business: construction contracts and concrete. In 1990, when he was forty-seven, he had the bright idea of setting up in business on his own. One day he was summoned to a meeting in Milan. He didn't think twice about it: he took his Lancia Thema, drove into town, pulled over to the side of the road in Via Lario and left the engine running. When two men on a motorbike rode up and one got off without removing his helmet, Laudari sat there quite calmly; they killed him with twenty-one shots to the head.

I still remember that execution. The newspapers said he'd been killed by some competitors, but the real reason for the murder was that he was too ambitious.

'Deception was Franco's magic. Once they decided to kill a *picciotto*, a guy on the lowest rung of the hierarchy; I can only remember his first name, Pepè. They spread a rumour, putting the blame on other people. They said Pepè had been trying to sell drugs in the Valtellina and that the locals had taken exception to this. At any rate, his body was never found; all they recovered was his Rolex and his T-shirt. They were lying on the edge of the lake, beside the road to the Valtellina. Pepè had vanished for good.

'The second rule is that of alliances. That was something Franco handled himself.' The boss had links with other bosses both in Lombardy and in the south. Every ten days or fortnight some criminal would arrive from Reggio Calabria, Crotone, Squillace or Castrovillari to hold some business meetings. For the drug trafficking in Comasina and the northern part of the province of Milan the key ally was Giuseppe 'Pepè' Flachi; whereas Buccinasco was the realm of Antonio Papalia, who provided logistical support for the supply of narcotics. The network extended as far as the Camorra, in the form of the Batti clan of Naples. This web of alliances enabled its members to share any information that emanated from the law courts and from informers within the police force as well as their political connections. It seriously worried other organizations like the Camorra, with which Franco had first built up a relationship and then, once he was properly established, fallen out with. From his humble beginnings running a bar in Lecco, by the 1980s Coco Trovato had come to be respected all over Italy.

'The third rule is family security. If one of his men was sent to prison, Franco looked after him and protected the interests of his family on the outside. He gave his children treats and paid his lawyers. He paid for everything without complaining.'

Blood ties, alliances and family security. These are the three reasons why it's so hard to find any member of Franco's organization who is willing to reveal the true facts about it. Only if a member of the 'Ndrangheta has lost contact with his clan – having fallen into disfavour because of some error, for example, or having been arrested and condemned to a long prison sentence – is he likely to do that. But even so, it's almost unheard of.

'There was one other important *pentito* in Franco's group, though, a close associate of his, but there was something I never understood about that case. This guy's name was Tonino, and he was known as 'o Scugnizzo. He confessed to over fifty murders when he had committed at least a hundred. Why did he forget about half of them? And yet it wouldn't take much to find out whether a *pentito* is genuine or fake. All you'd have to do is test his lawyer by suggesting that he defend someone who has turned state's evidence. If he agrees to do it, he's legitimate; if he asks for a lot of money upfront it means that he only accepts *pentiti* financed by the organization and that he's prepared to deceive the courts.'

•

The organization holds itself together through its hierarchy and its adherence to strict codes, but it depends too on centuries-old rituals. 'The first of these rituals,' explains Di Bella, 'is the "baptism", which gives you official entry into the family. It's the big step. The *capobastone*, the oldest member in the group, is taking a risk when he recommends someone, because if he introduces the wrong person he'll get killed too. If he, as *capobastone*, vouches for a person who later turns out to be an infiltrator, a *carabiniere* or a policeman, they'll kill him without so much as a second thought. By recommending someone for baptism the *capobastone* is indicating that in his opinion that person is a man of courage, of spirit. The recommendation for baptism is the last step in a journey. The *capobastone* is like a football coach. He goes into the bars and clubs, and if he sees someone he thinks has talent he puts him to the test. If the candidate successfully carries out the tasks they set him, he is approved for baptism. One kind of test might be to tell him, "Go to that stables; there's a horse worth 200,000 euros in there. Bring us its head." Or they might tell him to commit a murder. If he does it, he's proved that he's got the balls.

'The *capobastone* then decides, with the head of the family, whether the man should be baptized or not. A lot of people don't get baptized. Out of 1,500 men who worked under Franco or were close to him, about 500 were baptized; the others weren't but they were always ready, always hopeful it might happen. When they decide to baptize someone, he is summoned to a "sacred" place – a place where there's a statue of St Michael the Archangel, the 'Ndrangheta's patron saint. He then has to repudiate himself and his original family, his mother and father. The day you say, "Yes, I accept," it means that you accept the rules. You have taken an oath. If they order you to kill your mother, you must kill her. The crucial phrase in the ritual is: "May my flesh burn as this picture burns." They make you hold a picture of the Madonna or a female saint in your hand, while it's burned to a cinder. You must stand still even if you get burned yourself, otherwise you're judged unworthy. That's how you become an 'Ndranghetista. And you have to respect the code that begins with baptism and ends with burial. When a member dies he must be buried in the ground; he can't be cremated. You must return to the earth. We are earth and we shall be returned to earth. You are dust and you shall return to dust.'

Nobody leaves the 'Ndrangheta, alive or dead. Salaries and incentives are fixed according to your rank. If a member is killed, his membership is transferred to his family, whose everyday expenses are all covered. It is a kind of life insurance for the whole membership, and it makes the bond even tighter.

'In 2002,' Di Bella recalls, 'an unbaptized *picciotto* was paid 5,000–6,000 euros a month; a baptized one could earn as much as 10,000 euros after working for several years. In addition, he might get a bonus according to what he did, because if they gave him an important job to carry out he had a right to a further incentive. A *capobastone* got a fixed salary of over 20,000 euros and also had cover for his family: if you belong to the 'Ndrangheta and are killed doing your "job" your family is looked after as a matter of course.

'When you take the oath they undertake to maintain your family. For example, when Christmas comes they go round all the families of the organization and ask them for a contribution to help families in which the husband has died or is in prison. Money is provided for the wife, for food, and for the education of her children, but only on condition that these children later join the organization. If the widow says, "No, I want no more truck with the criminal world, I've had too much trouble already," she is released from the bond completely; she has no further obligations, nor do her children.'

Strict rules also apply to marriages. Di Bella goes on: 'If a member gets married he can't cheat on his wife. That's a law that you accept by agreeing to baptism. If they find out that you're cheating on her you're reprimanded, and if the wife appeals to them, if she names the husband's lover, they take steps. They go round to see the woman and tell her, "We'll let you off this time; but if you don't stop seeing our friend, on your own head be it."

'A lot of men do cheat on their wives anyway; even Franco used to say that a man had to sow his wild oats. He led his wife a merry dance (I can say that, because I knew his lovers), but he must have been discreet about it, or maybe his wife didn't mind.

'Women often play a role in the organization, too. If a woman has balls, they might give her restaurants to run, or prostitution rings. But women never had a position of authority in Franco's gang, even after his arrest. In the 1990s his sons and brothers ran things; his wife pretended that she didn't know what was going on, though in fact she'd known about everything right from the start.

'My wife never got involved. She didn't want to, and they didn't trust her. I used to tell her about many of the most dangerous jobs I did, but when I was offered the chance of a lifetime I didn't confide in her.'

4

POLITICAL INFLUENCE

The next time Di Bella calls he says he wants to meet somewhere new. Not the usual bar. Not at home. He decides on a shopping mall. 'We need a change of scene,' he explains. 'We need to go to a brand-new place, where the shops and bars have only just been opened. Where we've never been and nobody knows us.'

He summons us to a bar in a big Auchan mall on the outskirts of a Lombard town. The directions are precise. But three times we take a wrong turning. It's the agitation – indeed the fear – because all the precautions he imposes on us make us suspicious. So far everything has gone smoothly, and we've discussed some cases linked to famous names. But if Di Bella calls us four times from three different numbers there must be some problem. What is he afraid of? Does he think he's being followed?

The car park outside the bar is half-deserted. Had it been full we would at least have had an excuse to drive around in search of a spot and play for time. This way there can be none of that. Di Bella is already there, sitting at one of the three paltry tables outside the bar. His son is with him. Good. It's a good sign. Maybe. We exchange greetings, and the boy, silent as always, gets up and heads for a games arcade. Pippo is tense. We are tenser. His voice is hoarse and more monotonous than on other days.

'Are you OK?' he begins. We are, though maybe we'd rather be somewhere else. 'I told you to come here because it's quieter. I have to talk to you about some delicate matters. I want to explain to you how the 'Ndrangheta plays politics. You think: "OK, the politicians do a bit of conniving." You're wrong: it's the clans that run politics. They are active; the others, the professional politicians, are only passive. They decide things that the 'Ndrangheta couldn't care less about; if they do any different they're in trouble.

'I wanted you to come here because we need to look each other in the eye. When a state witness talks about the wheeling and dealing that goes on in Parliament, in the regional authorities and in local councils great and small, he has to be prepared to be attacked and discredited. They make you out to be a traitor twice over. I've decided: I'm going to talk. I owe it to my wife and my son. But I want to know, and you must tell me straight out because there's no going back, if you're ready. I need to know whether you're men of honour or whether you'll say yes and then dump me, or get me to tell you all I know and then not write anything.'

We can't quite tell if what we see in Di Bella's eyes is defiance or passion. But he doesn't even let us speak. He has already decided. The book goes on. And the story moves on – to Franco Coco Trovato's campaign to take over Brianza in the late 1980s. And he has some disturbing details to add to what was laid before the court during Trovato's trial.[1]

•

Perhaps surprisingly, the fact that Franco Coco Trovato was the 'Ndrangheta boss in Lecco was not widely known. The whole town should have known, but they didn't. At least not until 1992, when the big round-up of the Trovato gang saw Franco landed in prison for the rest of his life, serving seven life sentences. But before that how could anyone have thought that a man who owned several successful restaurants and drove around in a Ferrari was a mobster?

How could a person who had been given the Order of the Knights of Bethlehem by the local tradesmen's association be a mafioso? And it was not only Franco who was honoured in this way. His brother-in-law Vincenzo Musolino, who turned his hand to many trades, but was only good at one – laundering the Trovatos' dirty money – was also made a Knight of Bethlehem.

But until his arrest two years later, when the full story was revealed both in the press and in court, no one seemed to have realized that Coco Trovato might belong to the 'Ndrangheta. Indeed, that he *was* the 'Ndrangheta. Not even the fact that this model citizen, this respected entrepreneur, registered each and every one of his restaurants in the names of his wife and brother-in-law aroused the slightest suspicion. How could anyone see ulterior motives in such family loyalty?

There were clues, however, for those who looked hard enough.

Franco's favourite of all his restaurants was the Wall Street – a pizzeria that clan members called 'Five Stars' because it had one star more than the Griso, which was the most popular restaurant in Lecco in the late 1980s. The Wall Street was Franco's office. When his Testarossa was parked outside, you could guarantee that he would be there. He loved the place and was adamant that everything about it should be of the highest quality. It was a first-class restaurant, and if anything went wrong, it had to be put right. Immediately. On one occasion, a window got broken. Franco called his fellow businessman, the chairman of the Lecco Tradesmen's Association, Giuseppe Crippa, who had a factory in Olginate which made aluminium fittings.

Crippa was initially reluctant. After all, broken glass was not his problem. He supplied – and repaired – window frames, not the glass within them. Franco was livid. How dare Crippa contradict him? 'I'm going to come round there right now and show you.' He slammed down the receiver and jumped into his car. Luckily for Giuseppe Crippa, he couldn't find the address of the factory. Frustrated, but calmer, he picked up the phone again. This time Crippa was more respectful. Indeed, he took pains to make it clear that the respect and friendship that bound them must not be jeopardized over something as trivial as a window. The window was repaired. Franco was happy. And Giuseppe Crippa continued to provide fittings to both the Wall Street and Il Portico, another restaurant owned by the Trovatos in Airuno, also in the province of Lecco. Envious gossips among the local craftsmen couldn't understand how he'd won the contract, since the prices he'd quoted were higher than those of the other 'competitors'.

It should, however, be stressed that Crippa's relationship

with the Wall Street was purely a professional one – he was a supplier. He could not be expected to have known anything about Coco Trovato's shady dealings. And even though he appeared before the Court of Appeal in Milan, he was formally acquitted of any crime. Indeed he was amazed to learn that Trovato had any connection with the 'Ndrangheta. No crime, no guilt. That said, the court did censure the relationship between the former chairman of the Association of Lecco Tradesmen and the boss Coco Trovato.

But Crippa was not the only person who had never heard of 'Ndrangheta actitvities in Lecco or who had no doubts about Trovato's integrity. Local politicians exchanged greetings with him and went to eat pizza in his pizzerias. Where's the harm, after all, in dining in the restaurant of a model tradesman? Only one person persisted in thinking ill of him – the Lecco public prosecutor, Armando Spataro. Spataro found the eulogizing of Musolino and Trovato a little odd and ordered the tapping of Giuseppe Crippa's phone. It was he who intercepted the phone conversation between Crippa and Trovato about the broken window, in which the boss unleashed his fury on the leader of the Lecchese businessmen. It became a tiny footnote in what would come to be known as Operation Wall Street, an anti-mafia investigation originally launched by Spataro in

1991 and which would eventually reveal the extent of 'Ndrangheta involvement throughout the region.

By that point Lecco was front-page news all over Italy. The town woke up at last and realized that the 'Ndrangheta existed. And it was a shock: for the first time in Lombardy a charge of mafia-style criminal association was brought. But the investigation would take time, and until Spataro was in a position to arrest Coco Trovato, he and his family had an unassailable position in society. So, with the medal of the Order of the Knights of Bethlehem on his chest, Trovato (thanks to his wife) and his brother-in-law could walk around with their heads held high. Their noses were clean and they could meet anyone they liked. Including a new breed of emerging politicans.

•

A few weeks have passed since our meeting in the mall. This time Di Bella has chosen to meet us in his own home – it's almost as though he has dropped his guard – and his insights into Coco Trovato's links with the world of politics are, frankly, astonishing.

'The Northern League spoke a different language, but it was after the same things as the others: votes and power. And Franco, who had never cared two hoots about the colour of flags, understood much sooner than ordinary people that big changes were on the way. When Tangentopoli, the corruption scandal that changed the course of Italian politics, broke in 1992, I read about it in the newspapers, like everyone else; Franco had seen it coming years in advance. He'd started saddling the colt when it was still so small that nobody else would have dreamed of betting on it. He knew that if it later grew into a champion racehorse, he wouldn't even need to chase after it. It would recognize its master of its own accord and come trotting tamely back to him.'

Di Bella is in full flow, and even the smallest details float up to the surface from his memory. Unknown facts concerning the major political developments of those years, as well as completely unknown negotiations over votes for favours. Events that any journalist would love to write about, investigate and work on. Details that confirm that the 'Ndrangheta is no longer an abstract phenomenon, but an intricate spider's web that spreads over the whole of northern Italy. More questions, more answers. Then the bell rings twice in a row. Nobody speaks. The silence is oppressive. The kind where your heart slows down and seems to take on a life of its own; it beats so hard you can feel your pulse throbbing under your watch-strap. A third ring. 'Turn off the recorders,' he mimes to us without speaking. He picks up our bags for us, puts them into our hands, turns us round bodily and pushes us out onto the balcony. 'Stay out there and keep quiet until I come back.' And as he closes the French window and lowers the old blind, our protests of 'Hey, wait a minute' are cut short. Neither of us dares look the other in the eye. We are aware only of the sound of our breathing and a tingling in the fingers that clutch our computer bags. We are rooted to the spot. Not a sound comes from inside the flat – neither a reassuring sound nor a frightening one. Nothing. The flats across the road seem deserted. And even if someone were in them, what could they do to help us? Nothing. For the rest, nobody knows where we are, so how could they search for us? What an unpleasant place to die – a balcony no one has set foot on for months or years.

Then the blind rises again. Slowly. Too slowly, perhaps. We instinctively hold our breath. Then his voice, normal again, says: 'It's OK. Don't just stand there, come inside.'

'Who was it?'

'Nobody,' he replies. 'There was nobody there. We can go on, if you like.'

A nobody who'd rung the doorbell three times and who might come back. There's no way of eliciting an explanation. Di Bella wants to go on. We don't.

•

It's a week before we can bring ourselves to retrace our steps. We do so because what Di Bella has told us is extraordinary – and very disturbing. But it all remains to be verified. He has promised he can do just that, and today he's going to keep that promise. We're calmer now, and ready to listen.

Di Bella captures the atmosphere of the 1980s very well: the time when the parties of the 'First Republic' that was founded after the Second World War were beginning to break up at the national level. It was still several years before Tangentopoli, which would mark the end of the national five-party coalition of the Christian Democrats, the Liberals, the Republicans, the Social Democrats and the Socialists formed in 1981, and lead to the rise of Silvio Berlusconi and the beginning of the so-called 'Second Republic'. But in the north things were moving fast. In Lombard towns like Varese, Como, Bergamo, Lecco and Brescia, and in the Veneto too, people were excited to hear local politicians talk of secession. The idea of federalism was still a long way off, but there was widespread resentment about having to pay taxes to the capital. The first green-shirt rallies were held.

'Franco Coco Trovato had chosen to back the Northern League. If Franco had decided, there was no point in arguing. After all, what difference did it make to us whether the

Northern League or the Christian Democrats were in power? Our lives would be the same and more than likely our deaths would be too. Better to discuss the details of the theft of two big bulldozers in the Bergamo area. That was our daily bread, but the baker was Franco. He was the one who kneaded the dough. The only one.

'So I watched and listened and kept quiet. I was present on at least two other occasions when Coco Trovato reminded his companions – a sizeable group including Angelo Siri-anni, who would take over from him after his arrest in October 1992 – to vote for the Northern League and go around giving them good publicity. Which I did. I sponsored them, those northern bastards. I pleaded their cause with all the people I had any influence over. But on 6 June 1990 I didn't vote for them myself. It was a matter of principle. I didn't tell anybody, though. As Coco Trovato said, it was better to mind your own business.'

In the elections of 6 May 1990 the Northern League made a breakthrough: out of a total of 7 million Lombards, more than 1.2 million chose the League. In Como and Lecco the Northern League received 126,000 votes and became the second-largest party. In the meantime, Coco Trovato had gone to prison and made way for the new generation of 'Ndranghetisti.

•

Something similar may have happened to Angelo Ciocca, one of the Northern League's younger stars, who entered politics in 1996 and won the 2010 regional elections in the constituency of Pavia with about 19,000 votes. Despite his reputation as a highly skilled operator, Ciocca made a foolish mistake by shaking hands he should never have gone anywhere near. In the summer of 2009, when he was still a member of the Pavia local council, he was photographed by the *carabinieri* of the District Anti-mafia Office of Milan in Piazza Petrarca in Pavia. With him were three men: Giuseppe Neri, a lawyer, boss of the local 'Ndrangheta clan and a friend of Carlo Antonio Chiriaco, president of the Pavia local health authority; Antonio Dieni, a builder whose name appears frequently in the files of the Anti-mafia office; and Rocco Del Prete: at the time the campaign for the local elections was in full swing and, according to the magistrates, Neri was sponsoring Del Prete, who was running for a council seat as a member of the local party Rinnovare Pavia.

A few days earlier a phone call between Neri and Ciocca had been recorded. They had discussed a property transaction concerning a flat. Ciocca's meeting with Neri and the two other *compari* took place opposite the flat in question. They entered. A little while later they came out and went straight to a branch of the Monte dei Paschi di Siena bank.

What happened inside is not recorded. According to the anti-mafia investigators, however, the flat was sold to Ciocca at a bargain price to induce him to use his influence in favour of the candidature of Del Prete, which was opposed by the Northern League in Pavia. The election solved the problem, because Neri's man got 251 votes and was top of the reserve list of unelected members.

A year later, on 13 July 2010, both Neri and Chiriaco were arrested along with 300 other people in the biggest round-up of the Calabrian mafia that had ever been made in Italy. The inquiry was led by Ilda Boccassini, one of the best-known public prosecutors in Italy, particularly noted for her investigations into mafia infiltration in the north, and, more recently, into alleged corruption among the associates of Silvio Berlusconi. That compromising photograph of Ciocca's meeting with Neri was part of the mass of paperwork this latest inquiry produced.

Ciocca pleaded innocent and denied all charges. But the incident raised many questions. And not only in the heads of the electors of Pavia. Giancarlo Giorgetti, head of the local branches of the Northern League and Ciocca's political sponsor, evidently had his own doubts: because after the publication of the photograph he got into his car and drove to Pavia to meet Ciocca at the Lo Scoglio pizzeria. This was the evening before an important summit on organized crime in Via Bellerio in Milan, the headquarters of the Northern League.

Ilda Boccassini's investigation centred on one of the largest building firms in Lombardy: Perego Costruzioni.[2] For the 'Ndrangheta, being in control of Perego Costruzioni had at least three advantages: it enabled them to manage directly the earth-moving business, always one of the organization's favoured areas of business in Lombardy, to give contracts and subcontracts to allied firms and, above all, to control through an intermediary a business that would be in a position to win major public contracts, not least for Expo 2015, as the company outwardly appeared regular and above all suspicion

The offices of this firm were a point of contact between members of the *'ndrine* on the one hand and people employed by legitimate business, or even by the forces of law and order, on the other. One of the 'Ndrangheta operatives was Salvatore Strangio, an indefatigable boss who maintained the links between 150 Calabrian families and handled their business in the north through the Perego company. Strangio was heard in a wire-tap rebuking some members of a rival clan for talking too much, because they might attract the attention of the police: silence was crucial, he stressed, if you wanted to achieve your objectives. But he himself, in the same conversation, unwittingly revealed the

'Ndrangheta's aims: 'Perego,' he said, 'will win a lot of contracts for Expo 2015, but there are some people who don't understand that and create problems and confusion.'

Among the supposedly more legitimate figures involved in Perego, partly to keep rumours at bay – or so the 'Ndrangheta hoped – were Pietro Pilello and a member of the *carabinieri*.

Pilello was a successful accountant in Milan and had held a variety of public appointments which today might seem surprising: from the Milanese metro to the Milan International Fair. He had also been chairman of the auditors of Rai International and Rai Way, both divisions of the state-owned broadcasting company. Because of these directorships he had been investigated by the public prosecutor's office of Naples looking into alleged breaches of the law in connection with Rai Fiction, and features in their wire-taps.

The other man was no less a figure than the provincial commandant of the Vercelli *carabinieri*, who was alleged to have ensured that fines imposed on Perego's lorries for carrying excess loads (something they often did to maximize profits) were cancelled, and to have swapped tip-offs about phone-taps for an ultimately unsuccessful candidature in the regional elections. The official was charged by the Boccassini inquiry with being in league with the 'Ndrangheta. When the story was made public by the press, he replied through a blog, saying that his passion for politics was well known, that two criminals talking on the phone (as in the wire-tap that incriminated him) might say anything without the knowledge of the person concerned, and that he had met Salvatore Strangio, the boss who allegedly wanted him to be a regional councillor, only twice. Even the admission of those two meetings, however, is enough to send a shiver down your spine.

Some other big names from the Lombard 'Ndrangheta occur repeatedly in Boccassini's files. One of the small businessmen connected to Perego leads straight to Rocco Cristello,[3] a boss of the area of Monza and Seregno – Mariano Comense to be precise. Cristello is well known from numerous inquiries by the public prosecutor's office in Monza to have had close links with the Chinese mafia, so the appearance of his name in connection with Perego implies high-level collusion between the company and Chinese organized crime. It was deeply ironic for a party like the Northern League, which for years had made pro-tectionism one of its cornerstones.

•

But the Northern League was not beset by misfortune in Lombardy alone. In July 2010, at about the same time as the arrests ordered by Boccassini, Giulio Viale resigned as councillor in charge of the budget from the town council of Bordighera in Liguria. Viale had been a Northern League councillor for years, but when a report was sent to the prefecture which alleged collusion with the 'Ndrangheta, he chose to give up his post. Undoubtedly he was innocent, but for reasons of political expediency it was better that he stepped aside. Apart from the consternation caused by such accusations in Bordighera itself, Viale's daughter is Sonia Viale, Undersecretary for the Economy and a former aide to the Minister of Justice, Roberto Castelli. Better one resignation than the dissolution of the whole council on the grounds of infiltration by the mafia and giving favours in exchange for votes and a scandal that would reach the heart of government.

'Remember, we won you the election, so you can't say no,' was the 'Ndrangheta's motto in Bordighera as well as in Lombardy. And once elected with 'Ndrangheta support, no politician could back out of the relationship. It was a vicious circle.

There are other, similar cases. In Domodossola in 1993, the council of the Piedmontese town was dissolved, and an investigation began into three councillors, who were later convicted of criminal association. In 1995 the entire town council of Bardonecchia was dissolved as a result of a scandal over construction contracts. In this corner of Piedmont, the complex web of votes and contracts was dominated by the Mazzaferro family, a powerful Calabrian clan. The collusion between the Mazzaferros and the council had been going on for years, with votes going to councillors who would ensure that lucrative contracts went to firms favoured by the clan, but it was the Campo Smith affair that brought matters to a head. Campo Smith was a massive project to build a hotel and apartment complex and clearly had only one purpose: to enrich Rocco Lo Presti, the Mazzaferros' man in Bardonecchia. Just as in Bordighera and Domodossola dangerous friendships had originated with simple handshakes at electoral meetings, and innocent pats on the back had eventually led to handcuffs being clapped around wrists.

•

The next time we meet, Di Bella wants to talk about another aspect of local politics: the trade unions. It's a Wednesday morning. Again at a time when there is hardly anyone around. When we ring at the entryphone Di Bella doesn't even wait for us to speak: 'Yes, I know it's you. Come on up.

'My car is being repaired, I have to wait for the mechanic to find a second-hand spare part. In the old days

I didn't bother to take my cars to the garage; I smashed up one car after another. I was always buying new ones. Sometimes I'd keep them for a month, but never any longer than that. They guzzled petrol and they were fast. The only time I drove a saloon car was when I wanted to keep a low profile. I think about these things now that I have to drive a fifteen-year-old car; back then it didn't occur to me. I don't really miss the old days. But you can never turn your back on the past completely. There are certain people who are always criticizing the 'Ndrangheta but who would still be walking around in patched-up jeans, if it hadn't been for Franco.'

Who? More politicians?

'People who ought to be looking after the workers.' Di Bella points to our tape recorder: 'Turn it on.'

'Before Franco Coco Trovato came to power in Lecco the unions were barely functioning, just scraping by. They had hardly any money and worked in poky little offices. Then they began to benefit from Franco's favours – new offices, cheap rents, that sort of thing. I'm talking about the big three, the CGIL, the CISL and the UIL [Confederazione Generale Italiana del Lavoro, Confederazione Italiana Sindacati Lavoratori, Unione Italiana del Lavoro]. It was a clever strategy: Franco began from below, he was always prepared to be patient; he identified the most promising men in the various unions, the ones he could rely on, and he built them up, by ensuring they got the votes they needed, or by giving donations.

'Obviously the favours had to be paid for. And that was how Franco managed to infiltrate several of his own men into the unions. People he'd arranged jobs for in key companies. They then became union officials, which gave them influence over the other members of the workforce. Soon they were in a position to hurt the factory owners and, at the same time, clip the wings of any kind of protest against "friendly" businesses.

'In factories protected by Franco, the "real" trade unions didn't have any power. If Franco had an interest in a business and an employee made a complaint, he got nowhere. Nothing happened. Worse than nothing, in fact. Soon, either at work or outside the factory itself, in a bar, say, or a café, he'd be threatened, and if he didn't take the hint, he'd be running a serious risk: if he was lucky, losing his job; if he was unlucky, getting beaten up into the bargain. In "enemy" firms the approach was quite different. Franco would get the workers to start industrial disputes, to try to bankrupt the firm. It was a method that reached the parts that the protection racket didn't reach. The objective was always the same. At that time, if eight out of ten workers appealed to the unions, it meant closure, and that's what

Franco was waiting for. Once a factory closed down and the management was forced out, he could take over, either in person or putting one of his relatives in charge. He made money out of the industrial disputes too. They were a real racket. The clan kept a percentage of any money paid out to the workers by the employers at the end of a dispute. And money was always paid out. Because the threat of a strike wasn't like it is today, when it doesn't scare anyone. At that time a strike meant a mass strike. It brought the whole firm – even the smallest firm – to a standstill, and that was no laughing matter. So the workers almost always won the disputes, and Franco won too. He won three times over. Firstly, because he pocketed the money. Secondly, because he thwarted the union. Thirdly, because he either established a hold over the owners or drove them to bankruptcy.

'Thinking about how to control the factories by controlling the unions was typical of Franco. He was too clever to think only about the top people. He had friends everywhere. From the smallest town councils to the regional authority. He boasted about it. To tell the truth, sometimes he sounded a bit of a megalomaniac. "I've put people in politics," he used to say, "I've always done what I liked."

'There was a time, in the late 1980s, when every time we had dinner he'd start talking about the football club. He'd put a lot of money into Calcio Lecco. He had some way of transferring the money to a lawyer who was the official owner of the club and co-owner of a firm that manufactured light-bulbs, File S.p.a. The lawyer ran the club, because I don't think Franco knew much about football; it was more a matter of principle: being able to say, "The people of Lecco can't even organize their own football team without me." And in fact later, when the club was taken over by a clean company, Roda Acciai, it didn't do at all well – further proof that, although he was a braggart, Franco was usually right. It was the same when he talked about the women he slept with: everything he said was true. Or when he boasted about having men he could rely on in Mandello del Lario, Varenna, Abbadia Lariana, Ballabio, Barzio, Valgreghentino, Calolziocorte, Pasturo and all over the Valsassina. Not to mention Olginate.'

Di Bella worked as a bartender in Olginate for years and spent a lot of time there. Now he wants to tell us about his experiences there. All about them. To name names. And some of those names are quite surprising.

'In the good old days – good for us, I mean, 1983 and 1984 – the town had no more than 15,000 inhabitants, and half of them were southerners. Next to Lecco, Olginate was the place where Franco had the largest number of investments: restaurants, pizzerias and bars. It was like one big money laundry. And it was there that he was most in need of support in the local council. There was a trade unionist factory worker who was employed by SAE of Lecco, a steel firm. This man was very able. His name was Italo Bruseghini. He knew how to handle people and he'd known Franco for some time, though I don't think they'd ever done business together until then. But when the factory closed, he stopped being a worker to become a full-time trade unionist, and later became mayor of Olginate. Franco, who never placed a bet on the wrong person (except me, perhaps), gave the order, and the people voted en masse for Bruseghini. There were friendly councillors in Airuno and Calolziocorte too. But Bruseghini was different. In the first place he was mayor. What's more, when Franco was arrested in 1992, most of the local politicians dropped him. Even those who were themselves later arrested. But Bruseghini was different. Even after Operation Wall Street, he maintained his links with Trovato. I don't think he turned his back on anyone.'

We should make clear at this point that Bruseghini has never before been implicated in any judicial investigations. He himself has made the following statement.

I note to my surprise that on p. 78 [of the Italian edition of this book] it is claimed, with some emphasis, that in the 1990s Olginate was a centre for money laundering and the then mayor

– in other words, I – took a bribe to grant a licence to open a pizzeria.

I deny this, and deny that I have ever accepted money or other benefits from anyone. The truth is that Di Bella was never granted a licence, so he would have paid a considerable sum of money to obtain nothing. Moreover, I retired at the end of 1995, when the SAE was still active. I have never been a full-time or part-time trade unionist. I first became mayor in 1975 and I remained in the post until 2001, enjoying the trust and respect of all the towns-people. I wish to add that Dr Proietto is the magistrate who in late 2003 sent me notification that the investigations into events that had occurred in 1990–1 had been extended. The investigations were later dropped and I never received any further communication, nor was I ever questioned by the magistrate or by any other representatives of the judicial police. I can only assume now that the investigation was based on false allegations. I have always fought against organized crime. (Statements published by the *Gazzetta di Lecco* on 4 December 2010.)

Di Bella continues: 'In 1990 I was running the Bar San Carlo in Olginate, and after a few months I had the idea of turning it into a pizzeria. The premises had a restricted licence, and, judging from what I was told at the town hall, there was no possibility of changing it. So I went to see Mario Trovato. I briefly explained the problem to him, and he immediately advised me to speak to an Olginate accountant. When I went to the accountant's office, he already knew the whole story and said that this kind of thing needed "lubricating". Four or five days later he dropped in at my bar for a coffee: "I've been to the town hall. I suggest you pay a visit to the mayor." He emphasized the word "visit", to make his meaning quite clear and leave no room for doubt. "Would three million lire be enough?" I asked. He nodded and went out.

'I got the money, put it in an envelope, which I left unsealed, and got into my car. I drove to the office of the mayor's secretary, giving my name, then went into Bruseghini's office and filled him in on the subject. The mayor replied, "There's only one pizzeria in Olginate – 'La Sila' – so it is theoretically possible for us to grant another licence." He paused, then went on, "However . . ." I got the message. I produced the envelope and laid it on the table. The mayor opened it, counted the money without taking it out of the envelope and put it in a drawer. He sat in silence for a while, then said he hoped I'd bring him some votes in the next local elections and that he'd do his best.

'I felt like saying, "Are you serious? You're a friend of Franco and Mario Trovato and Salvatore Marinaro and you're asking me for votes?" I couldn't see why he needed my support, but I supposed extra votes were always useful in a small town. And he was as good as his word. A week later a big, burly policeman came to the bar and handed me some papers to be signed. It was so easy, because everyone in Olginate was part of the same network. But the fact that you've paid a bribe doesn't give you a lifetime guarantee. A few years later, I was forced to sell the San Carlo to Coco Trovato's sister-in-law. Business was booming, but I couldn't refuse. I consoled myself with the fact that at least he paid me eighty million lire as a token of gratitude and made sure that all my debts were cancelled. These things happen. You work hard, then you're forced to sell up. Never get too fond of any business, because they come and go.'

•

In Italy, there seems to be no escape from votes for favours. The practice is so widespread it makes you wonder if any other form of democratic expression exists.

In Trezzano sul Naviglio, Tiziano Butturini, the former PD (Partito Democratico, the main left-of-centre party) mayor and later chairman of TASM S.p.a and Amiacque S.r.l., the two public companies responsible for maintaining the water supply in the southern part of Milan, was arrested for vote-buying in 2010. Also arrested were the PDL (Popolo della Libertà, the main right-of-centre party) councillor Michele Iannuzzi, who until 2005 had been in charge of public works and ecology, the council's surveyor and a local entrepreneur. The latter was the vice-chairman of Kreiamo S.p.a., the property company which, according to the charges, was, on several occasions, given preferential treatment in the assigning of contracts by public officials. The warrants for the first three men came a year after a wave of arrests which had also affected the owners of Kreiamo: in November 2009 the chairman of the company had been arrested in connection with an investigation which led to seventeen members of the Barbaro-Papalia clan being accused of corruption, criminal association and a long string of other crimes. They were already in prison, having been convicted of other crimes, and all the properties registered in their names were confiscated. The inquiry continued and soon uncovered evidence against the councillors, the second tier of the organized collusion.

To give just one example among many, in Trezzano there was an area which seemed ripe for development, but planning permission was refused. So Kreiamo made out a cheque for 12,000 euros to Iannuzzi as an advance in exchange for an agreement to carve up the territory. The amendment was passed in February 2007, after which – although no evidence to prove it has yet been uncovered

– the balance of the favour, another 100,000 euros, must have been paid. And when Kreiamo went into administration in December 2009, some surprising off-the-books payments were discovered – a whole string of consultancies which bore no relation to anything in the real world.

Kreiamo was also involved in another important investigation into the Milanese 'Ndrangheta, which centred on the fruit and vegetable market. In December 2004 a consignment of 22 kilograms of cocaine was seized in a flat in Milan. This led to the discovery of an international drug-smuggling network, run by the Morabito-Palamara clan. This ring imported hundreds of kilograms of cocaine into the Lombard capital and invested and laundered the proceeds in a vast network of businesses and workers' and transport cooperatives, all of which were active in the wholesale markets. Eleven firms that operated in the fruit and vegetable market were raided. One of them was Sogemi, the firm part-owned by the Milan city council, which ran the whole area. One of the seventy people placed under investigation was a local police officer employed in the food-rationing section, the office that deals with the control of public shops and restaurants. Some employees of the licensing sector of the two Lombard town councils were also investigated.

What else could have shifted these mountains of money than votes for favours? The case has yet to be proved, but here too the name of Kreiamo crops up. Alfredo Iorio, the chairman of the firm, who was arrested in 2009, spoke on the telephone with the former councillor of Trezzano and listed three names of PDL politicians whom he intended to have elected. Iannuzzi replied: 'Then we'll draw up a list of councils we've supplied votes to, and I'll pay a visit to a PDL city councillor in Milan and present him with the bill for our expenses.' The phone call broke off at this point, but from the transcriptions by the Milan Anti-mafia Investigation Department the aim is pretty clear: the two men wanted a candidate 'of their own' to support in the regional elections of March 2010. It was impossible to achieve this through the complex party machinery, so they just checked through the list of candidates who were running and identified four. A trivial matter, you might think. Two small businessmen with a provincial politician, bragging about their medium-rank political friendships.

But the shadow of doubt is precisely the aim of the 'Ndrangheta, which always tries to pass unnoticed, like a chameleon. If you examine the facts of the case, however, the man behind Kreiamo was none other than Salvatore Barbaro, the son-in-law of Rocco Papalia, the old boss of the province of Milan. According to the Anti-mafia Office, Barbaro and a dozen district bosses met regularly on the outskirts of the city to discuss business, politics and votes for favours. And that was not all. Since 2006 they had discussed long-term strategies too. How do we know that? The killers convicted of the murder in 2006 of Giuseppe Fortugno, the PD vice-president of the regional council of Calabria, went up north to Milan before carrying out the operation. They made several trips, in fact. The last of them was on the day before they killed the politician. One wonders why they went to the capital of Lombardy on the eve of a major assassination. The theory the magistrates are working on is that they went to get authorization for the execution. It's a sign that the new Milanese mafia has plenty of poison to spread. And that in Trezzano, as in Reggio Calabria, elections were still an important hunting ground for the 'Ndrangheta.

After the regional elections of March 2010 a situation arose which would be hilarious if its consequences weren't so serious. On one side was the member of parliament Angela Napoli; on the other the regional councillor elect, Nino De Gaetano. Napoli wrote a parliamentary question to Roberto Maroni, the Minister for the Interior. She wanted him to check up on her colleague on the regional council, because 'De Gaetano's electoral campaign was run by Bruno Tegano and his wife in person.' The Teganos were old allies of the Trovatos. And Bruno's wife was the same woman who was shown on all television channels standing in the piazza outside the police station after the arrest on 26 April 2010 of her brother-in-law Giovanni (who had been living in hiding for seventeen years) screaming: 'He's a man of peace.' A man of mafia peace, maybe. One thing was for sure: either Napoli was a mad parliamentarian who made gratuitous accusations of collusion with the 'Ndrangheta or Maroni would be well advised to pay attention. Sure enough, a year later, on 5 April 2011, Bruno Tegano himself was arrested.

•

The threads of collusion are so fine that they're often invisible. The 'Ndrangheta permeates life in Italy, right down to the little local bakery, the restaurant that turns over a regular profit, or the one in the suburbs that serves only to produce fake receipts. Everything is grist to their mill, and nothing is underestimated. If the families need a helping hand there is always the town surveyor, or the legal practice that has made VAT fraud its stock in trade. In fact, there is a veritable army of officials and minor administrators ready to help the 'Ndrangheta and take a little share of the rewards.

'Bruseghini wasn't the only politician I paid in the course of my career,' Di Bella reveals. 'I gave money to many others. It happens. If you have to deal with the bureaucracy you inevitably have to pay. In 1995 I bought a restaurant in Cisano Bergamasco. It was a bargain, though there were some complications. The previous owner had falsified the papers of his predecessor. The restaurant was mortgaged, and there was a foreclosure hanging over it. Then the local *carabinieri* told me I couldn't open for business. So I went to see the director of Lecco registry office. I told him the story, and he wrote a letter, hardly bothering to look at me. It wasn't a real letter, but a sheet of paper with no heading and with some notes on it, which he told me to take to the head of the archive. I delivered it myself. The clerk looked at me and didn't ask any questions. He went away for about ten minutes and came back with a folder. It was the file on the original owner of the restaurant. He rewrote the whole thing in front of me. It was a long job, because he wrote it out by hand. But eventually he managed to backdate all the changes of ownership so that I could start the process of applying for a licence. It cost me three million lire [about 15,500 euros], but it was worth it. I recouped my whole investment in the first two weeks' work.

'Every town council had a particular speciality. In Malgrate there was the Tradesmen's Union. The mayor granted financing on easy terms – not to everyone, but certainly to members of our clan. In exchange he demanded a straight 10 per cent. In cash, of course.

'Then there was the Lecco Chamber of Commerce. From 1983 onwards the accountant and chairman Giuseppe Pupa had a very specific task, at least until Coco Trovato was arrested: helping friends and firms connected with the clan. I don't know how much he was paid, or indeed if he was paid. But I expect he was.

'Thanks to these friendships, my test for admission to the REC, the register of practising tradesmen, was almost laughably easy. I went to Como, because Lecco hasn't been independent, even in its Chamber of Commerce, since 1992. They asked me what ketchup, pepper and flaky pastry were. I was so bored by the whole process that I said I couldn't remember. The only time I answered was when they asked me what receipts were for. After the test a member of the committee led me out into the corridor. Five minutes later he came back to say I could go. I asked him if I'd passed. 'Go home and you'll see,' he said. Sure enough, a few days later my certificate of membership of the REC arrived. And the amazing thing is that it didn't cost me a cent, even though the usual price was a bribe of six million lire. Without the bribe and without connections, they made it really difficult for anyone to pass the test. There were environmental restrictions to be considered, and the distance from other restaurants had to be taken into consideration. You were actually supposed to know about all these things. It made REC membership seem like a mirage. Unless you had six million. But even then someone had to sponsor you, and that cost money too. The benefits of the clan can even be extended to non-members, as long as they pay up – through the nose usually – and never find out how wide the network of collusion is.'

Di Bella himself did people plenty of favours. There was someone who wanted to open a perfumery and needed a contact in the council, and someone who asked him to put in a good word to smooth the path of a building contract. 'I sent a lot of people to ask for favours, and made money out of it.' In this way, the 'Ndrangheta binds itself to a region, to its people, not just in the south, but all over Italy. It's a way of gaining respectability. Indeed, throughout Lombardy, in the many towns we travelled through while writing this book, they, the men of the 'Ndrangheta, are always considered 'above suspicion'. Whenever the police burst in flourishing arrest warrants, the first reaction of people who are interviewed about the suspects is one of surprise: 'He was such a respectable person.' When the authorities consistently fail to take any action against them, even criminals become 'respectable people'.

5

HOW THE 'NDRANGHETA GOT RICH

Of the 576 kidnappings carried out in Italy over a period of twenty years, from 1970 to 1991, more than 200 were the work of the 'Ndrangheta. Some victims were kept prisoner for a long time to push up the price of the ransom, others were killed after a few days and others were used for different purposes, in particular for entering into negotiations with the authorities. More than thirty simply disappeared. Most of the victims were from the north. Operations were coordinated by the clans that originated from the area contained between the towns Natile di Careri, San Luca and Platì, known as the golden triangle, because the clans from there made so much money. It was there that the terms of engagement were drawn up, and it was always there that all 'Ndrangheta kidnappings were initiated.

The name commonly used for this specific branch of the organization is the Anonima Sequestri. This was a term that had been used (along with Anonima Sarda) for groups responsible for various kinds of crime, but especially kidnapping, in Sardinia since the eighteenth century. These groups were particularly active in the latter part of the twentieth century, from the 1960s onwards. Later the term was used to indicate the same activity carried out by the 'Ndrangheta clans.

Kidnapping became a criminal way of life. With the proceeds the *'ndrine* bought mechanical diggers and bulldozers; they set up building firms, forcibly won public contracts and began the illegal devastation of many cities, towns and villages. In Bovalino, in the province of Reggio Calabria, there is a district the locals call 'Paul Getty'. It doesn't take much imagination to trace the origin of the name back to the grandson of the American magnate who was kidnapped by the Calabrians, or to guess what happened to the money from that kidnapping. But Bovalino is only one small example of what happened all over Calabria. Then, when the practice reached its peak, the clans of the triangle declared it defunct.

It was 1991, the year of the peace between the mafia bosses: the time when the *cupola* – the 'dome', the ruling committee of the local clan – was formed, which decreed that the clans should keep a lower profile. With a single shipment of drugs they could earn up to 3,000 per cent of their original investment, without any problems, without any fuss, without any roadblocks or patrols, all of which only impeded the 'Ndrangheta's other activities. The Platì triangle was in the vanguard, both when it launched the fashion for kidnapping and when it declared it to be over. It controlled everything, though its regime was not very strict; many members acted independently, which led to a series of clashes and bloody internecine wars in the period between 1975 and 1985.

The northern clans arrived with the second wave. They weren't true professionals – there were too many blunders – but the money came in anyway: at least 200 billion lire in the space of a few years, in the area between Genoa, Brescia, Milan and Varese. And the operations that produced this huge tax-free income were protected by *omertà*. Even kidnappers sentenced to life imprisonment would never reveal where the bodies of murdered hostages were buried. Anyone who is too talkative behind bars dies. So a constant flow of ransom money was ensured, and the northern 'Ndrangheta made a success of their new career. Kidnapping became a lever for exerting pressure on the authorities, for sending messages or even for blackmailing people who could pull the levers of official power. But before they reached that point, the clans spilled a great deal of innocent blood. Many of the kidnappings were badly planned and clumsily executed – especially those organized by Coco Trovato.

There's no pity, no compassion, either real or feigned, when Giuseppe Di Bella tells us about the kidnappings. Not a word for the victims deprived of their freedom and sometimes of their lives. So perhaps his memories of that time will offer some insight into the genesis of this indifferent violence.

'In 1975 Franco Coco Trovato already had a small army at his disposal, but he didn't have the rank or power of a *santista*. Those honours would come, but not until the early 1980s. After that he ruled as an "absolute dictator" over Varese, Como, Lecco and the Brianza. At the beginning of his career, however, he had to build a reputation as a hard man. And he committed so many murders that he managed that very successfully. Then, in the mid-1970s, he realized that he needed money – lots of it. And it takes time to make a billion by robberies alone. Robbery requires commitment and careful planning, and it's hard work, whereas with kidnapping you can make an enormous amount of money at a stroke. In 1975 a flat measuring 70–80 square metres cost 8 million. Imagine what you could do with a billion: buy a lot of drugs and become a major player in the organization.' And that was Franco's objective. So he decided to go into kidnapping.

In 1972 Pietro Torielli Junior, the son of a rich industrialist in the shoe-making business from Vigevano, was kidnapped. It was the first 'Ndrangheta kidnapping in Lombardy. He was released after the payment of a ransom of one and a half billion lire. It seemed like an easy way of making money, but it wasn't as easy as it seemed.

'The kidnapping itself is the easy part,' explains Di Bella. 'The problem is handling the person you've kidnapped. You have to find the right place, the right people. And quite a lot of them. And they must all be reliable. In Calabria it's not so difficult, because it's like an industrial process, a sort of production line. Nobody sees anything. It's not like that in Lombardy: even if you manage to find a suitable hiding place, there are still the logistics. And you need a team of ten people at the very least. But the main problem for anyone who is not a professional kidnapper is impatience. You have to wait months, if need be, before you get the money. When Franco entered the racket I don't know if he realized all this. From what I know of him, I doubt that he did. But when he got an idea into his head, there was no stopping him. So he started with the kidnappings.'

•

Cristina Mazzotti was the attractive, black-haired daughter of Helios Mazzotti, owner of a small cereal-growing enterprise in an area of Brianza near Como. On 26 June 1976 she had every reason to feel happy with life. She had just passed her school final exams with flying colours and she went out to celebrate with a couple of friends. She didn't even stay out late, heading home well before midnight. The three of them – Cristina and her friends, Emanuela and Carlo – were in the Mazzottis' Mini Minor. Carlo was driving. A Fiat 125 swerved in front of them and caused the Mini to stop. Three sinister-looking men in balaclavas climbed out of the car and shouted to the three friends to get out at once. One did the talking, the others pointed guns at the terrified teenagers. 'Which one of you is Cristina Mazzotti?' asked the first as he opened the door of the Mini. Cristina replied without hesitation. She was immediately dragged into the car in front, while the armed men tied her two friends up in the Mazzottis' car.

On 27 June, the day after the raid, someone called the girl's family and demanded a ransom of five billion lire, a vast sum that her father couldn't possibly afford – not even if he sold everything he owned. Then silence fell. For two weeks. On 15 July there was a second phone call. The price had dropped to one billion. Two weeks later the father paid up. But it would be a month before they had any more news of his daughter.

At the beginning of September, the *carabinieri* arrived at a rubbish dump in Varallino Sesia, in the province of Como, not far from Eupilio, the village where the Mazzottis lived. They had been alerted by a phone call which gave very precise instructions: to dig near the remains of a baby's pram. They found Cristina's body, covered by a few spade-fuls of earth and rubbish, under a broken doll. Her face, eaten by rats, was unrecognizable. The autopsy established three things. Firstly, Cristina had been dead for at least forty days. Secondly, she had been knocked out by massive doses of stimulants mixed with equally large doses of tranquil-lizers. Thirdly, when she was buried she was probably in a coma, and therefore still alive. Her murderers had kept her prisoner for about a month, perhaps already drugged up to the eyeballs, in a cavity dug in the earth near a farm at Galliate, before burying her in the rubbish dump. In the subsequent police raid, ten gang members were arrested. Their leader was Giuliano Angelini, a former fascist *squadrista* and arms smuggler, who had been a suspect in the Piazza Fontana bombing in 1969 and had a previous conviction for passing bad cheques. He was the owner of the farm at Galliate. The man who made contact with the Anonima Sequestri was Antonino Giacobbe, already known to the police for his involvement in kidnappings in Calabria. The logistics had been left to the small fry, which probably explains why the gang was rounded up so quickly. Giacobbe was placed under surveillance immediately because he had previous convictions, and in the six months after the kidnapping the others were identified through him. At the trial the following year, almost all of them were sentenced to life imprisonment, sentences which were later confirmed despite an appeal to the Court of Cassation. And even though he played no direct part in the brutalizing of Cristina, Giacobbe also got life.

And what of the man who asked during the ambush, 'Which one of you is Cristina Mazzotti?' Despite finding a number of fingerprints on the murdered girl's car, the initial investigation drew a blank. However, thirty-two years later, almost by chance, the prints were re-examined by Milan's forensic laboratory. This time there was a clear match. They belonged to Demetrio Latella, a drifter who had been linked to Angelo Epaminonda, a well-known gangster from Catania who was active in Milan. Years after the Mazzotti kidnapping, Latella was sent to prison for thirty years for murders unrelated to Cristina's disappearance and death. In June 2008, when he had almost served his sentence, the positive identification of his fingerprint finally nailed him for her kidnapping, and he confessed. It made little difference, however. The statute of limitations ruled out any prosecution for the kidnapping, and he was already on *semilibertà* – doing a job on the outside during the daytime and returning to prison at night. He told the police that he had kidnapped the girl together with two accomplices; and that he had done it on commission for twenty million lire. 'People I never knew, never saw, and who I've never had any connection with since.' No names, of course.

But according to Di Bella, the girl was kidnapped at the instigation of Franco Coco, a first cousin of Franco Coco Trovato: 'I'd known him for years. We did a lot of things together and got each other out of trouble on many occasions. There weren't many secrets between us. We used to discuss what we'd been up to during the week over a glass of beer. It was he who told me that the Mazzotti kidnapping was run jointly by Mario Trovato [the boss's brother] and Ciccio Parisi, who must be about eighty by now. Parisi was older than the others and had an honoured place in the gang, because he was the one who had started Coco Trovato on his life of crime. They were the prime movers and they organized the kidnapping. At first they wanted 5 billion lire, but they'd overestimated Mazzotti's resources. So to close the deal they accepted about a billion. It's still a lot of money, considering that they didn't even do the hard work themselves. Just as they paid for Mazzotti's daughter to be kidnapped, so they entrusted the job to a gang of small-time crooks who kept her under guard, then killed her. The 'Ndrangheta collected the ransom money, but the girl was already dead.'

•

After these early kidnappings, the clans realized that they could exploit their victims for purposes other than simple extortion. By singling out entrepreneurs, politicians and prominent local citizens they could send an intimidatory message to the authorities. It was not so very different from the messages the 'Ndrangheta send today, though now they use different means, such as a rocket-launcher hidden in a car outside the offices of the judicial authorities.

One of the first victims of this new style of kidnapping was a factory owner, who was held hostage for six months before suddenly being released. According to Di Bella, he was granted his freedom on one very precise condition: that he would give political support to the clan.

'It all began with a normal kidnapping. The usual plan: shifts for guarding the hostage, changes of hiding place, shopping only at a trusted supermarket and all the rest. But it ended with a stroke of genius. One of the 'Ndrangheta's many strokes of genius, in my opinion. If someone is your enemy, you kill him – that's reasonable enough. But why kill someone who might become your friend? The 'Ndrangheta aren't a bunch of shepherds who only live for their sheep and start shooting indiscriminately as soon as they step outside the fold. They take their time and think the problem through. They rationalize things: they think today I can make ten thousand but destroy the source of my income; better to earn five and invest in the future.'

And that investment might bring even greater rewards. Firstly, a consignment of drugs. Then, with the money from the cocaine, restaurants, bars, buildings and construction firms. And, lastly, lucrative public works contracts, which bring further profits with which the 'Ndrangheta buys more drugs, and the cycle starts all over again, growing bigger every time. It's difficult at first, but once the system has been launched, it looks after itself. Back and forth. Like the waves on the seashore. Except that in the case of the 'Ndrangheta the waves are made of money.

6

....

THE OTHER MAFIAS

There are two kinds of alliance in the 'Ndrangheta. One
is the alliance between your clan and the other *'ndrine*:
the mutual pact is absolute, so if the clan needs someone
murdered, that person is murdered – without question.
Then there is a deeper, more personal bond: that of being
a *compare*, or companion. A *compare* is more than a colleague, more even than a friend. Di Bella feels that we are
now *compari*, that we're bound to him by a tie of absolute
loyalty; it's the price for his confession. It's difficult to
explain to someone who doesn't belong to a quasi-military
organization based on a carefully constructed hierarchy and
who doesn't have a criminal mentality, but for Di Bella, the
belief that we are as one with him is a precondition. Without

it, he would not continue to tell us everything he has kept pent up for so long. We are the repositories of his secrets, secrets that can now, at last, be revealed. He has never before trusted anyone with so much. And it is that bond, that deeply felt loyalty, that underpins all the 'Ndrangheta's alliances. It is the basis of the relationships between the Calabrian and Sicilian clans – and those with the mafias in every corner of the continent.

'The turning point came in the early 1990s,' Di Bella says. 'The situation had changed for Coco Trovato, and for the other *'ndrine* and mafia organizations. In Milan the public prosecutors hit a lot of bosses hard. Including Franco. They didn't deal them a mortal blow, but it made some quick reorganization necessary. Also, new gangs moved into Italy from abroad: Albanians, Romanians – the Moroccans were already here – and Chinese. There was no way Franco and the others could have ignored them. Instead, what they did was recruit them. The new immigrants were helped to organize themselves so that they could run a sector of the business. They were effectively self-employed. With the increase in severity of sentences it was much safer to entrust the drug dealing to the Africans, while the Albanians were eventually given a remit first for prostitution and then for arms. The Slavs specialized in trafficking women and, if necessary, when accounts needed settling, acted as hitmen.

'Now,' says Di Bella, 'unless one of the clans wants to send a public message, the only organization that does everything itself is the Camorra. They fight among themselves because they're stuck in the past. As a result they make mistakes, and business suffers. They're not very good at delegating either. Not like the 'Ndrangheta. I can't help laughing when I hear on the television that a group of foreigners has decided this or is running that. It's complete nonsense. Do you think the Albanians just come in and start running the show? The idea's ridiculous. The 'Ndrangheta would wipe them out if they so much as tried. The foreign criminals survive and prosper because they're not really autonomous – and never have been. They're only autonomous in the eyes of the police. They're not the ones with the real money. They're in the pay of the 'Ndrangheta or, in some cases, the mafia.

'I didn't work that out for years, mind you. It took me a long time to put all the pieces of the jigsaw puzzle together. Back then I used to concentrate on my own stuff and I wasn't particularly interested in the decisions being taken over our heads. There was no way I was going to ask questions about the grand strategies.'

The pact with the Chinese mafia, however, is a different

matter. It was so sudden and wide-ranging a phenomenon that the members of Franco Coco Trovato's clan were specifically told that the Chinese were not to be bothered with threats of violence or attempts at extortion. It was early 1992: 'In February Franco, the Piromallis, the De Stefanos, the Papalias, the Annacondias and a group of Chinese met in a basement storeroom in Paderno Dugnano, near Milan. It was a dingy little place rented out to a street trader who sold clothes that had been stolen in the surrounding villages, one of those guys who do the rounds of the local markets.

'That afternoon he went out, and the bosses sat down to discuss how to share out the market in textiles, wholesale and retail clothing, pizzerias, restaurants and other outlets. They had authorization from the leading families in Sicily and Reggio Calabria. It wasn't just a local agreement, it was a big deal; they were carving up the whole of Italy. The process had begun four years earlier, almost by chance. Franco had started supplying batches of clothes to the Chinese, which they then sold on in Como and Milan. They're brighter and quicker than the North Africans (whom the clans had used before), and they made more money too. Soon they were making huge sums of money, not least because the Chinese were prepared to accept low profit margins in return for higher volume. They wanted to control the whole clothing sector. And all the 'Ndrangheta care about is making money.' The *'ndrine* always go where the profit is highest.

'So Coco Trovato kicked out the Moroccans and chose China,' Di Bella continues. 'Quite rightly, he said to himself: "If they're so good at selling knick-knacks and clothes, God knows what they'll be able to do with pizzerias, restaurants and bars."' The answer came in the space of a few months: 'In less than a year the Chinese showed him they were better at running the local bars too.'

It was the acid test, and Franco realized that this marriage would be a successful one, but only if the wedding took place at once. All he needed was a priest who was prepared to officiate. And in the storeroom in Paderno Dugnano, the De Stefano clan arrived to bless the union. The ring was put on the finger and, as should happen at all perfect weddings, the Chinese gangs and the 'Ndrangheta promised each other eternal love. The relationship endures to this day, and neither party has any intention of cheating on the other. For two reasons. Firstly, neither one side nor the other believes in the concept of divorce. Secondly – and perhaps more importantly – the relationship works so well that no other partner would be able to offer more: 'When Franco is involved things always flow downwards, just like water.'

In practice, it worked like this. Armed with a tip-off from one of their friends in the Chamber of Commerce or the Bankruptcy Court, Coco Trovato's men set the wheels in motion. The person in charge of maintaining relations with the Chinese gangs contacted his counterpart in their network and gave him the address of the tradesman who was to be approached with a view to taking over his business. His Chinese equivalent, in turn, identified the Chinese family that was to make the approach. This family then went to the tradesman and offered to buy him out. Except that the offer was 10, 20, often 30 per cent above the market value. And in cash. Just to make sure that they got the deal straight away and with no competition. The money, of course, didn't come from the Chinese: it was the fruit of Coco Trovato's money laundering and drug dealing.

The 'Ndrangheta's initial investment soon turned into a steady, fixed income. Each month the Chinese organizers paid the clan an agreed sum, usually 70 per cent of the profit. Trovato would send a young member of the clan to ask for a statement of accounts and to go through the books and the cash registers. If the business was turning over, say, thirty million lire, three or four million went to pay the Chinese who worked as waiters, chefs or washers-up while the contact, the Chinese '*capobastone*', usually got at least six million. The rest of the cash was put in an envelope and taken to one of the boss's deputies, who in turn passed it on to the boss. If the business already belonged to the 'Ndrangheta and all that was needed was a transfer of ownership, nobody paid when the deeds were drawn up. Either way, every month the agreed percentage – pure profit – was paid. It was up to the Chinese bosses to cope with any losses or any problems. 'Not that the Chinese were stupid – far from it,' explains Di Bella. 'The big fish of the Chinese mafia earned twice over: they took their cut of the profits and with the commercial cover of the bars and restaurants they smuggled a lot of illegal immigrants into Italy.'

For the 'Ndrangheta there were two advantages. The first was economic: their activities were no longer managerial but financial; the *'ndrine* either passed on the businesses or provided money to buy them from unwitting tradesmen, after which the Chinese returned the favour by paying their percentage every month. The second was almost greater than the first: the 'Ndrangheta no longer had to employ a labour force – no barmen or restaurateurs to run the businesses. The wider the clan's web, the more likely it was to break, whereas this way the Chinese handled everything. 'If the police and the *carabinieri* turned up,' Di Bella explains, 'it was the chefs and the waiters who got into trouble, because they were almost always illegal labour. And maybe the managers, who couldn't openly complain because their bosses kept a tight grip on their balls, and if anything went seriously wrong they blamed it on them. But usually, in the end, nothing serious ever happened.'

It didn't always work out quite that smoothly, as Di Bella himself testifies: 'In 1996, the first time I was arrested, I was taken to Bassone, the prison in Como. That same day about thirty Chinese were arrested. They were all put in one cell. Later I heard they'd been extradited. They evidently hadn't done their duty by their bosses and the 'Ndrangheta. But such disobedience was almost unheard of. Franco always knew how to make the relationship work – for better or, sometimes, for worse. If one of them stepped out of line, he'd be killed, but by the Chinese themselves, in front of everyone, to show that they were serious. The 'Ndrangheta didn't even need to get its hands dirty. Franco would say, "You've got to kill so-and-so because he's created a problem, and it's got to be public" So you'd take one of his compatriots, put a knife in his hand and order him to "execute" the guilty man in front of everyone. Four, five, ten stab wounds. And if the killer was arrested after the execution, there was no problem. Everything was taken care of. He didn't stay in prison long: the lawyers tried to get him sent back to China, and once he was there he only needed a friend in the police and, once the fuss had died down, he'd get out and be ready to come back to Italy and resume his life of crime.'

It was an infallible system, and it explains why the collaboration between the Chinese and the Calabrians was so effective, and not only in Milan and Lombardy, but also in Prato and the rest of Italy. Two years after that meeting in Paderno Dugnano, when Coco Trovato's empire seemed almost on the brink of collapse following the Wall Street inquiry, the relationship with the Chinese became even closer. The clan didn't die, it just washed its face. It laundered itself. And the Chinese were the soap: if there was even the slightest hint that a restaurant was at risk of being confiscated, it was handed over to the Chinese. 'I don't know if it's anything to boast about,' Di Bella says, 'but if there are Chinese all over Italy nowadays it's thanks to the 'Ndrangheta. And whose idea was it? Franco's. You've got to admit he was a genius.'

In the twenty years that have passed since, the system has been perfected; it has become all-pervasive, spreading through every kind of business, anything that turns a profit, both legal and, especially, illegal. The Chinese conquered Prato and the industrial suburbs of the Veneto. They specialized not only in catering, but also in textiles and import-export. They became leaders in counterfeiting. They invented a financial circuit tailored to their own requirements. They set up banks to launder the money and provide credit for the entrepreneurs who operate in the network.

Franco Coco Trovato's successful relationship with the Chinese was soon imitated by the other Italian mafias. Salvatore Giuliano, one of the oldest bosses in Forcella, in Naples, was the first member of the Camorra to admit making agreements with the Chinese. In the late 1990s, during questioning, he recognized Sun Shengde in a photograph. He was a restaurant-owner, a successful tradesman and a member of the Europe-Asia Chamber of Commerce. The boss claimed that he had an important role in an illegal smuggling operation involving containers.

In fact Shengde was soon eliminated from the inquiries: there was no evidence against the entrepreneur, who was a friend of the Chinese ambassador and in regular contact with leading Italian politicians. But the investigation did reveal reciprocal interests: the Italians fixed the final price of the goods and directed the commercial activities, while the Chinese used the services the Italian system could provide for getting round red tape and evading customs controls. That was how Chinese organized crime got its hands on Italy's ports. The Calabrian port of Gioia Tauro is a textbook example.

On 22 December 2009 the Reggio Calabria *carabinieri* arrested twenty-seven alleged members of the 'Ndrangheta and two Chinese citizens who controlled several important commercial activities in the port. The round-up netted bosses as well as ordinary members of the Molè and Pesce clans, some of them entrepreneurs with close links to the 'Ndrangheta. Even the former director of the customs office was implicated when the investigation revealed that the *'ndrine* were effectively acting as a customs agency. The *'ndrine* guaranteed their Asian partners not only the smooth passage of their goods, but a favourable rate of taxation, too. The Chinese made a profit in two ways: they sold counterfeit clothes at designer prices and, by declaring a lower price than the real one, they paid lower customs duties and taxes. They could save up to 80,000 euros per container, some of which went to the 'Ndrangheta as payment for their services and for 'clean' investments, which seemed to be legitimate businesses. The Chinese mafia made billions of euros a year in Italy, sending the money back to China using virtually untraceable methods.

The Guardia di Finanza have uncovered a vast number of illegal banks in the Chinatowns of Italy. The real number must be far higher. And in 2008 a single Roman money transfer agency investigated by the Finanza was found to have transferred half a billion euros to China. It's hard to say for sure whether it was all dirty money, but it certainly seemed suspicious. But the racket in the ports is small beer compared to the thousands of restaurants and small shops that are in the hands of the Chinese mafia. Not to mention the big shopping malls that they also control.

One of these, in Muggiò, Brianza, became the subject of a major investigation, and offers a telling illustration of how the alliances work. The arrests at Gioia Taura had shown how close the *'ndrine* and the Chinese importers had become, but the Cinamercato Brianza affair is perhaps the most interesting and colourful example of collusion between the different criminal organizations. It also shows how easily some of the Chinese bosses could reinvent themselves.

On 24 April 2009 the police arrested Felice Zaccaria. Zaccaria was the owner of Tornado Gest, a now bankrupt company. Arrested with him were his wife Aldina Stagnati, Saverio Lo Mastro, a businessman from Via Valentia, and one of the most notorious Chinese import-exporters in Italy, Song Zichai. The public prosecutor also brought charges against two other people: Stefano Firmano, a frontman used for illegal accounting operations, and Chen Honglai, Song Zichai's brother-in-law, who later disappeared in China. All of them were charged with fraudulent bankruptcy (a criminal offence in Italy), extortion and other similar crimes.

The story behind these arrests goes back to the early

1990s, when Muggio's town-planning department author-
ized the construction of a huge multiplex in the pleasantly
leafy area of Grugnotorto Park. The building firm, of
course, was Tornado Gest. Local residents started a petition
against the project and collected 2,500 signatures, but it was
ignored, and planning was approved. However, in 1998 the
regional council refused to give their consent, and it looked
as if the residents might prevail. But Tornado appealed to
the Regional Administrative Court and won. The following
year revised plans were approved, and in January 2005
Zaccaria opened the Magic Movie Park. But on 28 July, only
six months later, the multiplex closed. Predictably enough,
it had gone bankrupt. Soon afterwards along came Song
Zichai with his plan for a Cinamercato, a megastore selling
cheap – and for the most part fake – goods, modelled on
two similar outlets he had set up in Rome and Naples. He
was joined in the enterprise by two Calabrian businessmen, Saverio Lo Mastro and Rocco Cristello, who became
the leading figures in the affair. Through a new company,
Supercinema, the three men took over the multiplex and
bought Zaccaria's stake for five million euros, almost
exactly the same amount they had been paid in advance by
the Chinese tradesmen.[4] But in 2006 the cinema's licence
was withdrawn by the local council, and in January 2007
Tornado Gest was formally declared bankrupt by the court

in Monza. By the time Zaccaria and Zichai were arrested, the project had made losses of fifty-eight million euros. It wasn't a simple prearranged bankruptcy, and something had clearly gone badly wrong. Zichai, by being arrested, was literally saved from the hands of his furious compatriots. Rocco Cristello, the guarantor of the alliance in the eyes of the Mancuso clan[5] – the family from Vibo Valentia that was friendly with the Colombian FARC and had a strong grip on the province of Monza – was executed with twenty-two 9mm bullets while parking his car in Verano Brianza.

Although there are still legal proceedings pending against him, Song Zichai could have other surprises in store in the future. The son of an illiterate peasant, he arrived in Italy in 1995 on a false passport. Three years later he was arrested by the Rome police with an international warrant issued by the judicial authorities of Beijing. He was saved from the death penalty by the action of the abolitionist association Nessuno tocchi Caino (Let No One Touch Cain), which opposed the extradition. Zichai was released and began working in import-export, opening the Cinamercato Naples the same year. It soon had an average annual turnover of ten million euros. In 2002, Zichai, known to the Neapolitans as 'o Cinese (the Chinaman), bankrupted Palmese, the Serie C football club which he had bought; if the magistrates of Monza had not intervened, he would probably have done the same with Muggiò Calcio. Still in Naples, Zichai organized Maradona Night, a big concert by Gigi D'Alessio to be held in the presence of the Argentinian footballer in 2003. The tickets were sold, but Maradona himself never showed up. The audience was well and truly stood up. Strange to relate, the Chinaman disappeared from circulation for a while until he surfaced in Brianza, where he told a correspondent from a national newspaper that he was the future of Europe and of Italian business, no less. He has since served a prison sentence for the Muggiò fraud and is now at liberty somewhere in Europe. It wouldn't be surprising if, once the case has blown over, he reappeared in a few years' time in Veneto or Piedmont, perhaps under a new identity.

•

'Time passes, but nothing really changes,' says Pippo Di Bella, as he reaches the end of his account of the 'Ndrangeta's relationship with the Chinese gangs. 'On the surface everything seems different, but underneath it all, the way of making money remains the same. Now and again there are peaks of productivity or periods of crisis. That's when the inter-clan killings start. From the outside – I mean to anyone not involved in organized crime – that might seem like a very good thing: when I turn on the television news and listen to the headlines they always make it sound as if the authorities have dealt the 'Ndrangheta a devastating blow. I can't help laughing. The dry branches get lopped off, and people think they're the trunks.'

The same goes for the Asian mafia, which is as tough as all the other criminal organizations. In 2008 the Chinese started to step up their operations in Lecco again. They bought twice as fast as in the late 1990s, not least because in the meantime Mario Coco Trovato, Franco's brother, had come out of prison and was now running the clan. Initially, the *'ndrine* were dismissive of him: 'Not very bright, at least compared with his brother, and not good at handling people.' they said. But according to Di Bella, they've underestimated him. 'It's not true. He's very bright, he knows how to manipulate people and, also, he's nastier. More vindictive than Franco.' And at a time when everything was in flux, someone like Mario made a perfect boss. He kept things under control, and under his watch the Trovato empire, after several years of stagnation, grew stronger, while still following the path mapped out by Franco.

Every sector of the business was run according to the principles laid down in the storeroom in Paderno Dugnano in the 1990s: the clan would make others do the work, while they kept the profits. The clothing and catering operations were now completely in the hands of the Chinese, the drug trafficking in those of the Moroccans and Slavs. The Italians were left with extortion and robbery, especially from security vans. And robberies in the north were still covered by a pact made between the 'Ndrangheta and the Brenta mafia – so called because it originally formed along the River Brenta, though it later spread to dominate the whole of the Veneto and at one stage even Friuli – led by Felice 'Angel Face' Maniero. Even Maniero had come to an accommodation with Franco Coco Trovato.

'I was there when it happened,' Di Bella begins. 'It was in the spring of 1992. I met Sandrino, Franco's chauffeur, in the main square of Castello di Brianza. It was nearly midnight, and he asked me if I wanted to go to Brescia with him. He said he had to join Franco there to find out whether or not he needed an escort back to Lecco. I said yes, and we drove off in a Renault Clio 16v, although I don't remember now whether it was Sandrino's or Franco's. Anyway, Sandrino took the wheel, and he drove like a maniac – maybe because he had already sniffed half a dozen grams of cocaine before he reached the *autostrada* tollgate for Brescia Centre. He was famous for the incredible quantity of drugs he could take. Sometimes he drove around with a 100-gram packet in his car. For personal use, he used to say, and that was no lie. The upshot was that we reached our destination in barely an hour and a quarter, instead of the usual two hours plus.

'The rendezvous was in a sandwich bar in a tree-lined avenue, Via XX Settembre, near the flyover that links the railway station area with the district of offices and skyscrapers known as "Brescia Due". While Sandrino parked the car, I went into the bar. Franco saw me and raised his hand to indicate that I should go and sit somewhere else. I noticed that Angel Face was at the table with him. I returned the greeting and said, "I'll wait outside." I didn't fancy sitting at the table with someone like Maniero, if I hadn't been invited. You never knew. He might take it as an excuse to cause trouble, even though I had no idea what was going on or why the two of them were sitting at the table. I didn't want to get involved. So when Franco motioned to me to have something to drink or eat, I said no to that, too.

'As I was leaving the bar I met Sandrino and told him I'd wait outside, on the pavement. Sandrino made a gesture as if to say that it was all the same to him, and he stayed inside for half an hour. Then he came out, walked towards me and gestured to me to get moving. Franco and Maniero stayed inside, though. "How come he's with Maniero?" I asked Sandrino. "They're carving up territory,' he replied. So I suggested he leave me the Clio and stay with the boss. I knew Franco had come there in another car. I'd seen it parked nearby. But he said, "No, you came with me and you're going to leave with me."

'When we got to the *autostrada*, this time at the Brescia West tollgate, Sandrino took a whole packet of cocaine out of the pocket of his windcheater. I said, "What do you think you're doing? You've already got a hundred grams and you go and get another packet? Do you realize what this means, if they stop us?" But Sandrino was completely un-concerned: "Who's going to stop us? Don't worry about it." As he drove off, he opened the new packet, tasted it and said, "My God, it's good." And, as if to convince me that it was really quality stuff, he added that a new consignment was on the way. "They're bringing it from Brescia to Lecco. Franco and Maniero have made a deal."'

The packet was a sample of the consignment. And the deal was the beginning of a partnership that helped to change not only relations between the two bosses but also the balance of power between all the criminal organizations in northern Italy. That small consignment of cocaine marked the start of a harmonious relationship. For one thing, Franco and Felice got on well together, Di Bella recalls. 'They were about the same age. They both loved women. They were both show-offs. They drove around in Ferraris or Porsches and were always fashionably dressed. Maniero was already well known when I saw him with

Franco in the bar in Brescia; you could see he had balls.'
But he hadn't yet become a real boss. It was drugs that gave
him the opportunity to make the step up.[6] Although he was
made of the right stuff, he was out on a limb, surrounded
by a bunch of thugs who didn't have any clear strategy.
Gradually, though, he organized them, establishing a clan
hierarchy. Crucially, they were no longer content to stay
within the borders of the Veneto. They expanded into Friuli-
Venezia Giulia and Trentino-Alto Adige and then into
Romagna and Lombardy too. Soon, they had taken over the
whole of the north-west. They were good, too. Maniero
knew how to negotiate. He had the right friends in the
police forces. He paid well, preferring bribes to guns; he
only shot people when it was really necessary. Like the real
bosses.

Before the meeting in Brescia, Lake Garda had repre-
sented a very real border between the clans' territories
'Before 1992, Franco never went to the Veneto on business.
Afterwards he started moving across the border and opening a lot of restaurants and bars.' It was liberating; and it
meant more business and more profit. Maniero, for his
part, began to operate in Lombardy and Piedmont, special-
izing in drug dealing and robbing security vans. And Coco
Trovato decreed that such robberies on his territory should
only be carried out by the Brenta people. Previously these

hold-ups had been carried out by families of fairground operators – in Trovato's pay, of course. But there was no comparison. Maniero's people were professionals; they still run that area of business in northern Italy today.

But in 1995, Maniero was arrested and almost immediately became a *pentito*. He got a lot of people arrested and received a lot of favours in exchange. He had plastic surgery – paid for by the state – to change his appearance and he was given the funds to set up in business under a new identity. 'That was something that didn't normally happen to other *pentiti*, and I don't think it will happen in the future,' adds Di Bella. 'In our circles Angel Face was thought to be very lucky. The man who had everything. Mind you, in 2000 the Ministry of the Interior revoked his protection programme. On his daughter's eighteenth birthday, he had the bright idea of giving her a Porsche as a present. She started driving round the streets of Treviso in her luxury sports car with a police escort.' The newspapers got hold of the story, which led to embarrassing questions being asked in Parliament. As a result the protection service had to bring Maniero to book.

Strangely enough, it doesn't seem to have occurred to anyone to ask where he'd got the money for a car like that. Maybe he'd kept a cut of the money from the security-van robberies. At any rate, he was soon taken back into the protection programme. 'And he continued to live the high life on a pretty good salary,' says Di Bella. 'Some people get as much as 4,000 or 5,000 euros a month from the ministry, and have their grandfather, grandmother and grandchildren protected too. I don't think it's right, and I say that as a *pentito* myself. If I decide to turn state's evidence, it's only right that they put my family under protection: my wife and my children, if I have any children. Because my family's at risk as well. But the protection shouldn't extend beyond the immediate family.

'Anyway, Felice Maniero – and I heard this from a reliable source – found himself at this same crossroads, having to make a choice for his wife and children. His escort protected me too for a while, when I was living in the Veneto. So I could see for myself what went on.' Until 2005, Maniero had a small manufacturing business to which some of his former 'employees' were allowed access, working with it as suppliers or clients. They pretended to buy his goods, whereas in fact they were exchanging information about security vans that could be held up and other such 'business' operations. Just as they used to do in the 1990s, in the days of Angel Face's pact with Coco Trovato; the only difference was that the contacts were less frequent now. Trovato had been in prison since October 1992, but, through his brother Mario, he continued to run things.

'He's a born leader, a born boss,' says Di Bella. 'Maniero's like that too, and if you're a born leader you can't become an underling or give up altogether. It's genetics; nobody can go against nature. All you can do is adapt – you send messages from your prison cell, give orders from behind bars, for example.'

Three years after Maniero first entered the protection programme, the moneychangers of the Venice casino were still paying his gang their share of the proceeds. Which meant two things. Firstly, that the gang had not ceased its operations, and secondly, that its boss was still running the show.[7] But, just a few years later, in 2004, over 300 charges were brought against more than 140 members of the Brenta underworld. The investigation was based on Maniero's revelations, and had a profound knock-on effect. The members of the clan still at liberty were split down the middle: some men remained loyal to Maniero; but the rest formed a rival faction which would stop at nothing to gain power.

In January 2006 there was an attempt on Angel Face's life, which was thwarted by the police, but on 23 February his daughter fell to her death from a fourth-floor penthouse in the centre of Pescara. She had been living there under the name of Elena Marini. She was thought to have committed suicide. The next day Maniero, with his escort, drove down to Pescara to identify the body. He immediately declared that she had been murdered. It might be argued that it was hard for a father to admit that his thirty-year-old daughter had taken her own life. It would have been tantamount to admitting that he was, to some degree, responsible. But Maniero was certain; yet the official verdict was suicide and no investigation was ever carried out.

Di Bella continues: 'When I heard about the death of Maniero's daughter, Eva, I pricked up my ears. I thought straight away, "They've killed her to get back at him." A revenge killing. But no one had ever dared call Angel Face a traitor: he was too powerful. So I was surprised that this had happened now, so many years after he turned state's evidence. OK, he'd ruined the whole gang and incriminated hundreds of people. He was only dismantling what he'd built himself – in a sense he had every right to. So there must have been something else behind the girl's death.

'Some people I know decided to go to the funeral in the hope of meeting Maniero, but when they came back they said he hadn't been there. They were sure of it. But he was there all right. It's just that nobody could recognize him now. There's no doubt that he went to the funeral, accompanied by his escort. And I think he really wept for his daughter, who had paid for her father's faults.'

Four years before Eva Maniero's death, in December

2002, a heavily armed gang attacked a van just outside Ferrara. The van had three security guards, plus a police car which came to their aid; five men armed with handguns faced hundreds of Kalashnikov rounds fired by the bandits to cover their escape. The police realized that there must be another gang operating in the area, one completely unconnected to Angel Face Maniero. On 19 April 2004 they launched a crackdown. Arrest warrants were issued for 33 people, who were charged with 8 murders, 24 attempted murders, 16 hold-ups of security vans and 60 robberies from banks and post offices. The gang's objective had been very simple: to take over Maniero's territory.

The *carabinieri*'s primary target was the gang's enormous arsenal. Needless to say it was controlled by former members of Maniero's mob. After a three-year investigation, the police revealed that the breakaway gang used very specific methods. Each member had a clearly defined role, as in Maniero's original Brenta gang: the bosses decided what crimes they would commit and chose the new members themselves. Some of them provided 'clean' cars and found garages to hide them in; others had the task of spying out the land, checking on targets and tailing victims. The new bosses were also keenly aware of the obstacles in their way – two dedicated police officers determined to bring them down and, of course, their erstwhile boss, Felice

Maniero. It is hardly surprising, then, that Maniero was utterly convinced that his daughter's death was not suicide.

No doubt the new alliances will re-establish the balance of power in Veneto, as happened in Lombardy. The strength of the 'Ndrangheta and its associates lies in always being one step ahead. The *'ndrine* specialize in smuggling, certainly, but the true power of the mafias, especially the 'Ndrangheta, lies in their ability to think ahead. The 'Ndrangheta move slowly and plan pre-emptively. They can see that in five years' time it might be vital for Italy to have fast wireless connections to transfer computer and telephone data. They'll be sure to have acquired an interest in all the right businesses, ready to reap the profits. They reinvest the proceeds of their drug trafficking in 'clean' companies and double their takings. And to think that some politicians are so weak-minded that they're willing to serve the 'Ndrangheta for a few paltry euros.

7

THE ILLEGAL FREE MARKET: EXTORTION, THEFT, COCAINE

If you want to work with the 'Ndrangheta you have to think like a man of honour. But it's not enough to be a man of honour: you have to understand others' weaknesses and exploit them. 'It's only natural that it should be like that,' begins Di Bella, as we switch on the recorder yet again.

'If I think of my life, all I can say is that I've committed every crime in the book. But I don't feel like a god. I never have done. I've met some puny weaklings who after entering the family started to feel omnipotent and did their utmost to prove to the clan that they were just that. It wasn't like that for me. You have to be aware of your fear and of your limitations. We all have them. That's why I never got baptized. Because I like to think with my own head. If you swear undying loyalty, you can never say no. If they ask you to kill, you have to kill, and that's it. If they ask you to beat up your brother, you can't refuse. Of course, there are always times when you have to bow your head, but that's normal with all bosses. It's not just the 'Ndrangheta.

'At the age of eighteen, when I started earning my first money doing little jobs for Coco Trovato, I didn't know much about life. If it hadn't been for my father I'd have thrown myself into the organization heart and soul immediately. I'd have said yes to everything. But he forced me to keep my distance, at least outwardly. If I sometimes said no it was because of him, and they knew that. It was out of respect for him that they agreed to my, shall we say, part-time employment. I never thanked him, but it's because of him that I never got baptized, and, perhaps, that I'm still alive.

'In the early days I did a bit of everything; I only specialized later. My main contact in the clan was Franco Coco, Coco Trovato's cousin. He passed on instructions and set our objectives – people who didn't pay protection money had to be visited with a "request" that they pay their bill. At other times it was a question of beating up people who offended the boss in some way and who needed straightening out.

'Little by little, I became the gang's debt collector. From 1977 onwards that was my job. It always worked the same way: 50 per cent of what I recovered went to Coco Trovato alone, 40 per cent (it varied from case to case) to the person who was owed the money, and I got the rest. On top of that, in addition to the percentage I received on the money recovered, I got a fixed salary every month, about a million lire. It wasn't very much, but it didn't matter: there were extras. I might have become a specialist in extortion and debt-collecting, but I hadn't given up my other activities. Besides, the 'Ndrangheta doesn't have employees: even if you're paid a full-time salary you're still effectively a freelancer. You can take initiatives, get involved, make use of what you know. Trust me, I learned how to exploit every last piece of information I got from my time as a security guard.

'Of course, now and then things went wrong. But as long as you kept to your own rules you'd be OK. One of my guiding principles was to let people know that if I said something I meant it. Another was not to be too greedy – that was my motto really, and I always stuck to it. Especially when I started to be – even though I say it myself – a pretty smooth operator, first in arms smuggling and then in the cocaine business. Though that's a delicate subject, because I don't like drugs. Whenever they're mentioned it sends a shiver down my spine. I don't like them and I never will. They're the ruin of the clans. Nowadays all mafiosi are as high as kites from dawn to dusk. They do the stupidest things at the slightest provocation. Then, the next day, they don't even know what they did. And then I think of my son; I can't bear the thought of him taking cocaine. Not to mention heroin. That stuff brings nothing but death, and it hurts the clan, too. If you kill your customer with lethal drugs, what kind of tradesman are you? There are some lines you don't cross, in work or in life. It always ends in trouble if you do.

'I don't think I've ever crossed the line. Not even when I made the daughter of a woman I used to live with marry a Moroccan. Not that they really became man and wife. It was a sham marriage, of course, though they went through the official ceremony in the town hall. I told the girl she had to marry a guy who needed a residence permit. It was only to earn a bit of money. His name was Muhammad El Alami and he came from Fes. He'd been in Lecco for some time but he was an illegal immigrant. I told him, "For 6,000 euros plus expenses – you'd have to pay the expenses, of course – you can become an Italian." There was nothing wrong with that. Sure, when I was arrested the judge wanted to sentence me for that too. But it was nothing, a trivial matter. It was only 6,000 euros. But every little bit helps. It's like when you're playing cards. If you sit out one hand, you're liable to lose the whole game.

'But apart from small jobs like that, my main task was always extortion. I did the other jobs to earn a bit of extra cash and maybe even to have a bit of fun, to liven things up. In some ways, I was like an accounts clerk. The process was always the same. Some member of the clan would call you up and tell you to do a collection – usually you'd be talking about twenty or thirty million lire. Rarely more than a hundred. It was a daily routine. You leave home at nine in the morning and get back at ten in the evening. You go to the debtor's home. You ring the doorbell. The wife answers the door and always says, "My husband's out, he'll be back when he finishes work." Usually at seven thirty. So you while away the day. Then an hour before the agreed time you turn up again and wait. In 98 per cent of cases the collection goes smoothly. At other times you realize that the lemon has already been squeezed dry. So either you throw him out of the window, but that way you don't get the money, or you change tack. If, after you've kept an eye on him and seen the kind of flat he lives in and the kind of car he drives and how he dresses, you realize that he's a family man in deep trouble, it's best to adopt the gentle approach.

In the first place, never raise your voice or talk about debts in front of the wife. Or in front of the children. A man will find that offensive. Some things should stay secret. Besides, it's a matter of respect for his family. I don't even want to imagine how I'd react if somebody made a scene like that in front of my son. I'd either be furious or depressed. Either way it's no good. You'll never get money from someone if you put their back up, and a person who loses their self-esteem won't make the effort to find the money. So you've got to put him at his ease. And sometimes the best thing is to show him that you're reasonable: you tear up the IOUs and say the debt is paid. It only takes a second. You tell him you don't want to harass him and he needn't worry, he won't have any more problems. Then you make a note of his phone number. A month, even a year may pass, and you go round to see him again. Because nothing is free and, one way or another, debts must always be paid. Maybe there's a tip-off from his office or a word in the ear from a neighbour. You can be sure that, partly out of fear, partly out of gratitude, you'll always get any information you want. You then either use it yourself or you sell it on.

'But if you get an order from the bosses to put the squeeze on someone and take possession of their assets, it's a different story. Then you have to demand "real" money – and you keep going back: 100 million lire becomes 600 million, and your victim just can't pay any more. So you threaten him until he's willing to sign over everything he's got. You make him sign a bill of sale; an accountant or lawyer connected to the clan takes care of the paperwork and puts everything down in black and white.'

Di Bella's matter-of-fact account doesn't stop at the theory. When he starts to fill in the real names and places it becomes even more shocking: 'Remember that accountant I mentioned. He was based in Valmadrera and he managed about ten condominiums, a third of which he owned himself. I don't know what he'd done wrong – perhaps he'd refused to sell a property the clan wanted – but since the order came from Coco Trovato himself, I didn't ask any questions. I knew we had to scare him and make him sign a wad of documents that had already been drawn up. Franco, the boss's cousin, and I waited for him across the road from his house, where he usually parked. He drove up around midnight, and we went over to him and invited him to get into our car. He didn't try to resist. He thought we were out to rob him, but we put him right, then drove him to Lecco and took him out onto the iron railway bridge over the Adda. When we got there we gave him a couple of punches in the face, tied a 20-metre rope round his ankles and lowered him slowly down from the parapet into the water. We could see fairly well in the moonlight: we put his head underwater for about a minute and then pulled him up to let him breathe for another three minutes. He started screaming, louder and louder. We repeated the process about ten times, until he gave in. By then his voice was so shrill it sounded like a woman's. He promised to do anything we asked him to do. Of course, we wanted the buildings.

'When we finally pulled him up he was soaked in water from head to waist and in something else at crotch level. I handed him the pen, and Franco got out the papers. He signed everything. We drove him home as calm as could be. Later I heard he'd been cleaned out; he was left with hardly a single property to his name.

'He had no other choice. If he hadn't accepted the clan's proposal we'd have let him drown. We didn't have any choice either. If we'd let him go free without those signatures, we would have paid for it. And not with money.'

•

The Lecco law courts are a friendly place. So friendly that if you're a member of the 'Ndrangheta you'll find doors will open for you. In 2007 two employees of the bankruptcy section, three businessmen and a lawyer were arrested. The arrests marked the end of Operation Noose, a Guardia di Finanza investigation into loan-sharking. The investigation had first been triggered in 2005 by a complaint from a member of the public about two car salesmen. The father-and-son team Pietro and Antonio Colombo were in the habit of waiting for the right tip-off about a struggling businessman, for whom they would then underwrite loans at interest as high as 180 per cent. The evidence against them was overwhelming, and they agreed to talk. They cleared their consciences by giving a full statement, in which they incriminated dozens of people, all involved in a clandestine financial racket. It was a completely parallel world, undercutting Lecco's legitimate businesses and ideal for laundering money. Thanks to the lines of inquiry suggested by the car salesman, the Guardia di Finanza hunted down the head of Lecco's bankruptcy department and a bailiff. The public prosecutor's office claimed that they were in the pay of the racket. The circle seemed to have closed.

But, thanks to the testimonies of two *pentiti*, it was soon revealed that the racket was even bigger than had at first been thought. The circle had not closed at all. It had simply doubled in size. One of the *pentiti* was Danny Esposito, who, before he turned state's evidence, ran several firms on behalf of Coco Trovato, who, as we've seen, continued to keep a close eye on his business, despite being behind bars. With the help of one of the men who had just been arrested, an accountant, Esposito set up a system of false invoicing and carousel frauds, disguising them as sponsorship for three local football clubs: Calolzio, Olginatese and OlimpiaGrenta. The other *pentito* was Di Bella. He was able to give the Finanza a rundown of the dynamics of debt collection. He knew the system well – for years it had been his daily bread. In this particular case, he revealed that two of his friends had collected the money for the Colombos, Vincenzo Falbo and Maurizio Agrati.

In the files of the Como *carabinieri* there are detailed profiles of four of the 'Ndrangheta's key contacts in the Lecco area. The officers of the provincial HQ deemed Agrati to be the most dangerous. He was no mere debt-collector; no pawn of the racket. Quite the contrary: he was the armed wing of the Coco Trovato clan, a key player in the development and 'well-being' of the clan, effectively 'crowned' by Coco Trovato himself. In the mid-1990s, when Di Bella worked more closely with him, he ran the clan's drug-smuggling operation, the perfect training for becoming a boss. It was the kind of springboard reserved for the brightest and most ruthless men. And he succeeded, despite being arrested and sent to prison. As we have seen, prison bars don't automatically restrict a man's freedom of action.

Taking the lid off this particular racket revealed quite a lot else, besides.

It emerged that Colombo senior had also been a crony of Agostino Rusconi, a friend and partner in crime of Di Bella's, who had been killed in 1998. And another name that cropped up in the numerous strands of investigation thrown up by Operation Noose was that of Antonio Schettini. Schettini was the namesake of another Antonio, nicknamed 'o Scugnizzo, Coco Trovato's trusted killer and liaison officer for the clan's contacts with Giuseppe 'Pepè' Flachi throughout the 1970s and 1980s. He was also a friend of Jimmy Miano, the expert in clandestine gambling dens who for years acted as an intermediary between Angelo Epaminonda and his fellow townsman Nitto Santapaola. But Schettini was also Coco Trovato's grandson. And here the circle really does close. The same names keep coming up. The same rackets are exposed. The cancer of crime spreads and changes shape. The more it is attacked by judicial inquiries, the stronger it seems to become. It is almost as if the 'Ndrangheta grows every time it is cut back. The authorities think they are digging up the roots, but in fact they are just cutting off a branch. They prune it; instead of repressing the organization they stimulate its growth.

The same happened with Operation Wall Street. There was a heavy crackdown, with nearly 140 arrests. A veneer of legality was spread over the whole territory run by the Coco Trovatos. So much so that, nearly two decades later, some politicians are still boasting about that investigation. But the magistrates behind Operation Wall Street know only too well that not even the subsequent round-ups – Operation Countdown and Operation Final Act, in which the next generation of *'ndrine*, notably Coco Trovato's son, Emiliano, were arrested – were enough to clean up the area. And these just scratched the surface. One could go on and on – there have been more than ten major investigations in Lombardy alone.

Luckily for Schettini, he was only marginally affected by Operation Noose and its successors. The same was true of Angelo Battazza, too. Battazza was a businessman who was well known throughout the Lecco area in the 1990s and is still well known today, thanks to his links with football. Battazza was accused by Colombo, the car salesman, of being part of the secret *cupola* in Lecco. However, there was no evidence against him, no crime that could be laid at his door.

But what does Di Bella say about him? 'I know Battazza very well. In 1994 we met, or rather clashed, in his office in Olginate. At the time he had at least forty lorries. He was trespassing on the territory of another Lecco firm, Brambilla S.p.a., which specialized in transport and logistics. The owners of Brambilla weren't just annoyed, they were livid, because they said Battazza owed them a long-standing debt

– about 100 million lire. The Lecco people called Rusconi and asked him to intervene. Agostino came round to see me, and we set off together to do our job.

'The office was deserted. There was nobody there apart from Battazza. I didn't greet him; in fact I didn't say anything at all. I roughed him up straight away as a preliminary warning, and Rusconi said, "Wait for us. You know who we are." He knew, all right. In fact, you might say he knew us better than we knew him. We never went back to his office for the second appointment. Neither Rusconi nor I had thought to carry out a check before knocking on the door of his office. I don't know why. We usually did: we checked whether the person could be touched or was protected. But that time we hadn't done it, and we soon found out that he worked for the Trovatos. We'd made a mistake, a bad mistake. A member of the gang told us to stop hassling Battazza at once. Then the boss's cousin Franco confirmed our orders. We immediately backtracked and made ourselves a lifebelt: we got the Brambillas to pay us by signing over some flats they owned and we used the rent from one of them to cover the expenses of clan members who were in prison. The Brambillas didn't make too much fuss. But I'd like to have seen them try. We'd done the job. It wasn't our fault that it hadn't had the intended result.

'We were just in time: the day after we'd made the

Brambillas hand over the flats, I was in a bar in Olginate when Mario Trovato walked in. He was fuming with rage. He came over to me and, without worrying about who else was or wasn't in the bar, slammed me against the wall. He shouted so loud I couldn't understand what he was saying. He probably called me a fool. But obviously I wasn't going to ask for an explanation. It didn't seem like a good idea. Luckily, I was saved by two things. Firstly, I'd been in the gang as long as Mario had, and he knew I was trustworthy and that I wasn't trying to cheat him. I didn't say anything. I let him rant on. When he eventually calmed down, I explained to him that the Brambillas had paid us with property and that there would be some for him too. Obviously a larger share than we'd have given him if things had gone as expected. In the end Rusconi registered one flat – the one for the prisoners – in his own name. The other two went directly to Mario Trovato's sister and niece. So we managed to solve the problem that way. In the end, as long as you're bringing in the money, nobody will touch you. But it certainly takes a lot of work.'

•

The investigations into loan-sharking brought to light a new aspect of the 'Ndrangheta's activities in northern Italy.

They were, in effect, using the commune of Campione d'Italia, which enjoyed certain tax privileges not shared by the rest of Italy, as a vast money-laundering operation. Campione's unique position as an Italian enclave within Switzerland makes it a perfect place for anyone wishing to wash their dirty money. That it boasts the largest casino in Europe only adds to the attraction. It offered a ready supply of desperate victims for Lecco's crafty loan sharks, who used the moneychangers operating outside the casino to find new markets and to clean up their illegal profits. The gambling addicts were victims twice over: of themselves and of the 'Ndrangheta.

The moneylenders didn't lend money only to people who lost at the tables, but to anyone who needed money and couldn't get a loan from a bank. That may be the reason why the casino of Campione has been targeted countless times by the magistrates since the early 1980s; yet it is still open and still performing its valued role in society. Especially criminal society. The State Auditors' Department periodically reprimanded the town council, but that was another cry in the wilderness. Contracts were awarded on the basis of a handshake, and some expenses weren't put on the balance sheet but in a safe place, or rather places – overseas tax havens, significantly, on the island of Sint Maarten, in the Dutch Antilles, or in other small Caribbean states where people of the calibre of the Santapaolas and Spadaro – top-level mafiosi – own casinos and simple transit holdings. Coco Trovato, too, had men at the Campione. They are probably still there.

'In Campione d'Italia,' Di Bella explains, 'Franco had a contact. For many years Delta [code name of a person who might be the subject of new investigations] ran pizzerias and restaurants in the area between Oggiono and the Val d'Intelvi. But they were only a cover. His real job was money-laundering. He was good at it. He possessed an encyclopedic knowledge of financial operations and money-laundering and had friends everywhere – not only in Campione, of course, but in all the border towns, including Como and Lecco. Delta reported to the boss, and when Coco Trovato was sent to prison he continued to report to his son Emiliano and then to Mario Trovato. He was an important person; you could tell – he was treated like a prince. Both in the clan and outside – in the chambers of commerce, for example. In fact, at the Lecco chamber of commerce, he was treated like a king. Of course, there were lots of Franco's men there, including Giuseppe Pupa. He was an accountant and the chairman of the chamber of commerce. In fact, he was the one who had arranged my membership of the REC, the register of practising tradesmen, for virtually nothing and, in 1986, he'd introduced me to Dino Guida: through him I got the best deal of my career – he gave it me on a silver platter.

'Guida was also an accountant, based in Albavilla, but he worked all over the Lecco area. For several years he had specialized in buying and selling property. Actually the term "buying and selling" is a bit of a misnomer, because hardly anybody bought or sold anything. The business deals he brokered were mostly scams. His speciality was building terraced houses and medium-priced flats. Nothing luxurious. He'd collect all the deposits and when he thought he'd got enough – at least 30 per cent of the advertised price – he'd keep the money and declare himself bankrupt. Then he'd be ready with a new frontman to start a new building project. So when Pupa introduced him to me I already knew where the conversation would lead. I was good at debt-collecting, and Guida dealt in large sums of money. Ten to one he wanted me to collect something he was owed. I was right. It was no less than a billion lire. Pupa told me to go to Milan to see a senior manager who worked in publishing. And to handle it any way I liked. He gave me a note with the address, and I saw that the address was in Segrate.

'I went over there three days later, and Nino Miraglia, Nino Macaone and Nino Parisi, Ciccio Parisi's grandson, came with me. All three were from Lecco, and I'd known them for a long time. They were trusted people who worked for Coco Trovato. The address was a handsome office block, next to a filling station. When we got there, Parisi waited downstairs. I went up to the fourth floor with the others. I was carrying a briefcase which contained all the tools of my trade and, most important of all, the IOUs. When we got up there, all the assistants were at their desks outside the managers' offices. It was nearly lunchtime, and I asked to speak to our man, saying I was there on behalf of Dino Guida. His secretary went into his office and when she mentioned the name I saw the guy jump up from his desk. He told her to send all the other girls away: "You can all start your lunch break early." He had sensed that something was up. But I didn't give him time to think. When the last secretary had gone, I gestured to the one of my associates, the one closest to me, to block the doorway. Without saying a word, I punched the guy in the face, and he shouted, "Don't hurt me! What have I done to you?"

'"You've let Dr Guida down and you ask me what you've done wrong? Here are the IOUs. There's a billion to pay. What are we going to do about it?"

'Despite everything, even with three of us standing there threatening him, he tried to be clever, shouting: "It's him I owe money to, not you."

'I just shouted back – even louder. "No you don't, we've bought the debt." In fact that was rubbish: nobody buys debts. You read about such things in the newspapers and hear about them on TV, but nobody really buys debts. If anything, it's quite the opposite. No criminal would take on a debt unless he was sure he'd get the money. When a debt is collected, it's standard practice for the collector to keep up to 60 per cent of the sum. You have to cover your expenses, too. Petrol, a meal in a restaurant. You have to tail your quarry, check how many times he goes out for a coffee. If he doesn't pay up, or pretends to have forgotten the debt, you might have to kidnap his children or his wife for a while. And that's expensive. There are a lot of costs to be covered. Naturally, though, your profit is always exclusive of expenses.

'This guy can't have known much about how these things work, because he didn't reply. He just stood there goggling at me. But I knew how to wake him up. I took a bottle of methylated spirits out of my briefcase and started pouring it over the furniture and the table. I was bluffing, of course, but he fell for it. He seemed genuinely scared and begged for mercy. He asked if he could spread the payment over two instalments.

'"Oh sure, next time we'll pay you a more leisurely visit, maybe we'll even sweep out your office for you, and to thank us for the favour you'll have the cops here waiting for us," I said to him. He was a classic type – scared of physical pain, but underneath it a double-crossing shit. The kind of guy who will whimper to your face but try to get you as soon as you're a safe distance away. I insisted on the billion. I sat down and waited. Without saying a word. He did the same. Every now and then I repeated the word "billion", without taking my eyes off him.

'The two Ninos who were covering my back kept quiet. Then suddenly I flicked open the two locks of my brief-case. The noise made him tremble, as though I'd primed a revolver. But then he wrong-footed me: "In that case I don't know what to do. Go ahead and kill me."

'There was no point in killing him – we wouldn't get the money that way – so I said, "Listen carefully. I know where you live and I know all about you. I know your working hours and I know you like your coffee without sugar. Let's say two instalments, I'll accept that. But you've got to pay me the first one now."

'He had a small safe in his office, which was in full view. It was already open, in fact. He took out 250 million. Can you believe that? He'd been snivelling away and he had all that cash in his safe. Anyway, I didn't bat an eyelid; I put the money away in the briefcase. I made a sign to the others, and we left. I gave the briefcase to Miraglia and followed them out. As I got to the doorway, the manager took me by the arm and asked me in a whisper – so that the others wouldn't hear – when we'd come back.

'"Have the money ready. I'll let you know when we get here," I replied.

'Two weeks later we called on him again. The same team as the first expedition. But when we arrived outside the entrance to the building, there was something wrong: the street sweeper was working too hard to be a real street sweeper and there were various suspicious-looking workmen standing around some manholes, where they'd put up a safety barrier. In other words, the place was crawling with cops. I turned on my heel and went to the nearest phone box. I had the extension number of the office, it was written on the IOU that Dino Guida had given me. I dialled the guy's number and told him in no uncertain terms what I thought of him. I hung up and then I met the others at the central station – we had a plan B, needless to say. We were all furious; if he'd been there with us I don't know what we'd have done to him. Nino Miraglia said, "I'm not going to let him get away with this. I don't care if I go to jail but this guy's fucking us about and he's got to pay for it." He was right. But it was better not to do anything for the moment.

'We all went back to the San Carlo, my bar in Olginate. From there I called Guida and tore into him, too. When you get a sense that things might go wrong it's important to make the person who hired you feel guilty. Put him a situation where he feels that his life might be in danger: "Listen, you bastard, you're going to write a statement saying that I'm acting on your instructions as your employee. That way, even if I find the *carabinieri* waiting for me, I won't give a damn because I'll be there legally to ask for your money. You'll be sending me. And I'll have the IOUs in my hand."

'The next day Guida wrote out a statement authorizing Signor Giuseppe Di Bella to act on his behalf. And I went back to Segrate with my usual three-man backup. It was after lunch when we got there, and I went up to the office alone. When he saw me, the manager turned pale: "It wasn't my doing." For all I knew he might have had a tape recorder under the table, so I pretended to be puzzled. I said, "I'm sorry? What are you talking about?" And he said, "When the four of you came the first time I gave you 250 million lire, and then the next time there was that trouble with the police." Again I pretended not to understand and kept up the performance: "My name is Giuseppe Di Bella and I've come as the representative of Dr Dino Guida of Albavilla. He sent me about these unpaid bills of exchange." And I showed him the wad of IOUs. I went on play-acting until he calmed down. I explained that there was no need for him to worry and that if he didn't have the money I'd call some other time. I let him accompany me to the lift and then, when the doors were about to close, I pulled him inside. I could be certain we were on our own there. I stopped the lift.

'"What have you done, you bastard? You've miscalculated badly, because if you have the four of us arrested another five will come and they won't be as gentle as we are. I know what you're trying to do: you managed to trick your friend Dino Guida, and now you're trying to trick us. And that is not acceptable. You and I are going to go back upstairs and you are going to keep your mouth shut and give me some more money." Without a word, he opened the safe again and took out 300 million. Then, a month later, he paid me the rest of what he owed. The full billion.

'The other three had been hired by the clan, and they got their money from the Trovatos, while I kept 180 million. The rest I took to Franco, because if he found out I'd raised that sort of money without telling him, I'd soon be found dead in a skip. Besides, he was owed some of it by rights for his protection. I needed that protection the next day, when I went round to see Guida. I bawled him out. I accused him of sending me to someone who was untouchable because he was connected to a powerful family: "You sent me to ask for money that couldn't be asked for." The performance had its effect: Guida was clearly convinced that I hadn't succeeded in collecting the debt. Or maybe he wasn't really taken in but realized I was working for someone who it was better not to argue with and who had kept his cut of the proceeds. "Leave me the bills of exchange and I'll see to it myself," he said in a whisper. I took the bills of exchange and tore them up in front of his eyes.'

•

All 'Ndrangeta bosses need to keep control of their territory – not just in terms of drug running or instilling the right level of fear into people. One of the primary means by which they keep control is by offering a valuable service – protection.

It can be a very expensive service. The *pizzo* is calculated and applied to any asset and any person who lives in the relevant area. It's like an insurance policy, except that the person insured doesn't decide when to take it out, doesn't know the terms and conditions before he signs the paperwork and hasn't a clue how much it will cost. On the other hand, there are no exclusion clauses, and when a claim is made, your word is enough to ensure that it is paid – in full. And the terms are never altered; there are no regional variations – it doesn't matter whether you live in Lombardy or Calabria. The *pizzo* is the same in Milan as it is in Reggio. Moreover, the premiums don't go up every year, so you always know where you stand.

On 19 July 1982, just before 1 a.m., Cosimo Morelli was killed in Reggio Calabria. He was a fairground worker who 'earned' his living stealing cars, part of a gang of travellers that had been hanging around the Modena area of the city for some time. He was at the wheel of his Alfa Sud, the car was stationary, the engine was switched off, and his girlfriend was sitting on the right-hand seat. A motorbike with two riders drew up alongside. The one on the pillion pulled out a pistol and fired several shots. He wounded the woman and killed Morelli.

Two days later the Reggio flying squad arrested a scrap dealer from Condofuri. His name was Antonio Cento. The police had a file on him, and when his photograph was shown to Morelli's girlfriend she identified him as the killer.

Shortly before the murder, Antonino Labate, who lived in Modena, had woken up one morning and found that his Fiat 127 was missing. He'd reported it stolen. But not to the *carabinieri*. Instead, he'd gone to Francesco Zincato, the local boss, who belonged to the Libri clan, which controlled much of the city. Zincato had immediately guessed what had happened and summoned Morelli. He'd asked him to do him the favour of recovering the stolen Fiat 127. He knew perfectly well that Morelli was probably the thief, but adopted this respectful approach as an opening gambit. The respect was evidently not mutual, because the car did not return to its place outside Labate's house. It was found by the *carabinieri* on the Salerno–Reggio Calabria *autostrada* the day after Morelli's murder and three days after Labate had officially reported it stolen. He had eventually reported the theft to the forces of law and order, but only after getting the all-clear from Zincato, who had had to admit that he hadn't succeeded in recovering the car.

This was humiliating for a man who prided himself on controlling every inch of his territory. And on 11 September, two and a half months after the theft, two more fairground workers were caught in an ambush in Reggio Calabria. Pasquale Libri, the clan boss's godson, was accused of attempted murder and was alleged to have used the same gun that had killed Morelli two months previously. It all added up: he was clearly the other man on the motorbike. Or rather, it all seemed to add up. When the trial began, it emerged that, although Libri had indeed tried to injure the men, he'd done it because they'd refused to give him free admission to the fairground on the evening before the attack. The trial also revealed that the gun used to kill Morelli was not the one that was used by Libri for his revenge attack. The envelopes containing the evidence had been mixed up in the court archives, and in the end it was impossible to tell which were the bullets from the earlier murder and which were the ones from the more recent attack. Lastly, it turned out that the dead man's partner was extremely short-sighted. In the witness box she retracted her earlier identification of the killer, saying she was no longer certain of what she had seen. The prosecution tried their best, but in the end the judges acquitted both Cento and Libri's godson.

Years later, in 1992, statements from a *pentito* called Giacomo Lauro shed new light on the case. Morelli, he said, had been killed on Zincato's orders as punishment for his lack of respect. In the first place he'd stolen a car in an area of the city – Modena – that was protected by the clan. Then, when he'd been politely asked to return the car, he'd ignored the request. In the eyes of the clan, the appropriate penalty was death. The result of the trial, too, was predictable: all the accused were acquitted. The 'Ndrangheta toasted its success and closed the circle.

'When it comes to controlling a territory,' Di Bella observes, 'the *'ndrine* have to guarantee payment. Doesn't matter whether it's in Calabria or in Lombardy. "Guarantee" is the key word. Sometimes they threaten and sometimes they provide the other party with a *pizzo*, an insurance policy in effect.

'As I've said, when I was young, I did go to collect the *pizzo* once or twice – but no more than that. But when it was a question of putting the squeeze on a tradesman, I was more than happy to go. The *pizzo* is always calculated on a business's real takings. The clan are not like the tax people: they don't let the hidden earnings slip through the net. If a shop or restaurant has a declared turnover of 10,000 euros and the organization knows its real takings are 40,000, the *pizzo* will be a percentage of that 40,000. After all, Franco's gang run bars and restaurants themselves, so they know down to the last cent what the turnover in a particular town or district is.'

The 'Ndrangheta don't need to carry out detailed research, or trawl through the audit the way the *fisco* – the Italian tax authority – does. Instead, they put a shop under surveillance and by the end of the month they know the exact number of its customers, both regular and occasional, its turnover and the quality of the goods it sells. Provided they don't want to squeeze the tradesman too hard, all they need to do is calculate the profits and cream off 25 per cent of that sum.

It's not just a one-sided relationship. There are advantages for the tradesman, too. If a 'foreigner' – which can mean anyone from an area not controlled by the clan – carries out a robbery in a protected shop, say, the clan's machinery immediately goes into action. The delegate for that area or town, having received the 'report' on the robbery, investigates and asks a few questions: 'How many of them were there? How tall were they? Did you see the car? What time was it?' The order goes out to look for anyone who was in the area at that time and hadn't requested authorization. The robbers are almost always caught at once with the loot, which is of course returned to the shopkeeper.

'Franco had contacts with gypsies, fairground workers and fences. As well as corrupt policemen and bribable *carabinieri*,' explains Di Bella. 'If a "friendly" patrol stopped the robbers, they'd immediately inform one of Franco's men and hand the robbers over to the clan. If they'd taken them to the police station the loot would certainly have disappeared or been confiscated, and that would have been the end of it. The organization's strength is based on speed – and the corruption of the law enforcement agencies.'

That swift response and an unerring ability to find the right person to bribe is a very powerful combination. It's also what enables the 'Ndrangheta to enforce the *pizzo*, no matter how high the price. Sometimes, it can be a real bloodsucker: for instance, if a business looks like it would be a strategic asset for the clan, its owner becomes an obstacle. So the *pizzo* collector raises the percentage every month until eventually the owner is forced to declare himself bankrupt and gratefully accepts a transfer of ownership. 'It usually doesn't take more than six months,' says Di Bella.

•

Every year at least 1,000 thefts of heavy machinery are reported. The items stolen include mechanical scrapers, shovels, diggers and lorries. These machines are much sought after, because it's easy to dispose of them in eastern Europe and the southern Mediterranean. No more than 20 per cent are ever returned to their owners; the other 800 vehicles disappear without trace.

Today it's no longer sufficient just to remove the numberplates, as it was in the 1990s. Even in the Maghreb the authorities carry out careful checks. Or at any rate more careful than those they carried out a few years ago. But as long as you remove a few parts and change the chassis number, you'll be all right. In 2010 the *carabinieri* broke up a gang in Chivasso, not far from Turin. The ringleader was caught in the process of dismantling the vehicles to prepare them for the North African market. It's risky and it takes time, but as long as you have a few warehouses where you can park the machines, you shouldn't have any problems.

Once you've made the modifications you transport them via the *autostrada*, getting through the tollgates by using stolen Telepasses. By the time the highway police have noticed, the lorry the machine is being transported on has already reached its destination.

The following is Di Bella's account of a big operation to steal some bulldozers. The process was unbelievably simple.

'The best work opportunities always seem to come along when you're trying to relax. In early 1993 Rusconi and I met a group of Tunisians in Lecco. They hung around the same bars as us: the Belfiore – the one near the Wall Street – and some others in Bellagio. You'd see them from about ten in the morning onwards. Sometimes they'd be playing on the machines – the videopoker games in the bars, infernal machines that devoured all your money. I never went near those games. I stuck to billiards – traditional cues and no flashing lights, and I only played in the afternoon.

'One day it was colder than usual. I went into a bar in Calolziocorte with Rusconi. Their leader – he called himself Franco – was there with two of his mates. I persuaded Agostino – who usually wouldn't play – Franco and one of his friends to have a game of *boccette*. Nothing serious, just a way of passing the time. After about a quarter of an hour they suggested we do a job for some other Tunisians who lived in Genoa. It involved stealing quarrying and earth-moving equipment in various parts of Lombardy. Rusconi looked at me; his eyes said yes. He was brilliant at that kind of silent signal and now he gave me to understand that he needed an assistant. We agreed to do it.

'We all made a lot of money out of it. And it wasn't just one lucky strike. We carried on for nearly five years, and Rusconi never failed. Wheel loaders, backhoe loaders, exca-vators and quarry dumpers. Each theft was commissioned as much as a month in advance, because they wanted specific vehicles with particular features. The first request came in March: they needed two 15-ton bulldozers, used for clearing the ground before laying a road. They're diffi-cult vehicles to transport, and there was another, more serious problem. The owners often fitted the bulldozers with satellite-based alarm systems, because the machines cost up to 400 million lire new. So we had to go round a dozen building sites before we found the ones we were looking for. One was a six- or seven-year-old Fiat Allis near Caravaggio. The other was a Komatsu. We found it parked ready to clear the ground for a car park in Segrate. Neither had a satellite-based burglar alarm. Perfect.

'So, after we'd stolen a lorry equipped with a heavy-duty trailer, we got to Caravaggio at around three in the morning and by 5 a.m. we'd loaded the other one too, the Komatsu.

At nine o'clock we were just entering Genoa. The handover took place in a service station near Nervi. They gave us half the fee up front: 80 million lire. We pocketed it and asked for a lift to the station so that we could catch a train back to Milan. Three weeks later, the Tunisian sought us out to give us the other 80 million: the previous day he'd received a box containing the numberplates of the two vehicles, proof that the bulldozers had reached their destination safely. He told us his colleagues in Genoa had sent the machines by ship to the port of Tunis.

'When the vehicles arrived in Tunisia the numberplates were removed. Then they loaded them onto some other lorries and took them to Libya without even needing to change the chassis numbers. At other times they transported the machinery by a longer route. They sailed from Genoa as before, but made a detour via Barcelona. I think the destination was still Tripoli, though I can't be sure about that: in our business you were often told that something had been ordered by people in Palermo, then later you'd find out that in fact they'd been from Naples. That's fair enough. You have to do a bit of disinformation. It's a matter of security. We did it ourselves, and you can be sure the Tunisians did too. Maybe the machines ended up on an Algerian building site rather than a Libyan one. Or in some other, completely different part of the world.

'What I said about the numberplates is true, though. When we sent a few small excavators to some Calabrians based in Lugano, before we transported the machines we had to dismantle them and change all the serial numbers of the spare parts. We had to put on fake ones, otherwise it would have been impossible to use them in Switzerland, let alone get them through customs. In North Africa nobody bothers about such things. Partly thanks to that, our business went smoothly, at least until the summer of 1998, when Rusconi was killed. At that point I gave up. I had no choice. He was really expert at handling heavy machinery, whereas I can't even drive those brutes, let alone steal them.'

•

The 'Ndrangheta's core business, however, is still drugs. All the other businesses revolve around them. They are complementary or subsidiary. They serve for laundering or reinvesting the vast amounts of cash which cocaine, in particular, brings into the coffers of all the mafia organizations. But it's the *'ndrine* that dominate the sector. And it's the Calabrians more than all the others who have a constant need to find new systems and new covers to launder tens of billions of euros.

When the clans are under pressure, discotheques and nightclubs are too conspicuous, and it is in the 'Ndrangheta's interest to get their hands on ordinary bars and pizzerias, even bakeries or patisseries – businesses that don't usually attract attention. The quantities of drugs are enormous, so the clans need an equally large number of places for storing, cutting, repackaging and distributing them. Shops make excellent fronts. Who would ever suspect that a patisserie was a front for a seedy trade in cocaine? No one. Apart from a few public prosecutors like Marcello Musso of Milan. Musso proved – and he was the first to do so – that the sale of a kilo of bread in Mariano Comense or a croissant in Giussano helped to finance the 'Ndrangheta's drug trafficking.[8]

The gang connected to Giampiero Modafferi and Angelo Mondella, who were already known in Germany for drug smuggling, concealed the sale of cocaine originating from the port of Gioia Tauro behind the mask of a dozen harmless-looking shops. They reinvested the proceeds in property, both in Lombardy and in Calabria.[9] In Pontetresa, near the Swiss border, the Guzzi clan combined bread-making with smuggling and arms trafficking. In Pieve Emanuele, in the province of Milan, there was a baker's shop which served as a front. And for those who didn't even want to pretend they were working, there was the option of running videopoker games. At least 30 kilos of cocaine a month arrived, via various routes, in Lecco alone, and from there it was sent out to other towns in Lombardy. The price of most of the drugs was fixed in Milan – not just for Italy but for the whole of northern Europe. The fact that there was no conflict about pricing and costs suggests that any differences between the clans had been set aside in the interests of profit. Progressive cartel agreements were established between the various organizations, which relied on groups of Maghrebis and Egyptians for the retail selling. There was a constant interweaving of transnational interests. Di Bella gave us a good illustration of exactly how it worked.

'In March or maybe April 1995,' he says, 'Maurizio Agrati called Agostino Rusconi and said he wanted to see him. Agostino asked me to go with him to watch his back. That evening we met him in Cesana Brianza. The next day a group of Turks was due to arrive in Lecco to bring some drugs they'd bought in Amsterdam. We had a brief meeting. They handed over the bags of hashish to Maurizio, who paid them on the spot, then we all went our separate ways.

'There were six or seven Turks and about twenty of us. Agrati had mustered quite a few people, too, because he wasn't sure if he could trust the Turks. And about 500 kilos of hashish were involved. So we did our bit, in the knowledge that there'd be a share for us too. Three hours before we were due to meet we walked round the car park and right round the block. Then we repeated the circuit every half-hour, until twenty minutes before the meeting. A nice, easy patrolling job which, since everything went smoothly, earned me 11 million lire. That was the way I liked it, when drugs were involved. I preferred that kind of job. It was cleaner. Sometimes I had to buy drugs and sell them on, even though I wasn't keen on it. But you can't always do what you like. At least I had the advantage of being able to go straight to the source when I had to buy cocaine.

'My supplier was Bruno De Luca, Coco Trovato's brother-in-law – which was virtually the same as being supplied directly by the Trovatos. In fact once when I made an appointment to go to De Luca's house I found Franco's son Emiliano there. He'd come round to deliver six or seven packets of cocaine to his uncle. I didn't count the packets. They gestured to me to go into the garage under the house, while De Luca quickly cleared away the stuff. Then we went back upstairs, and Bruno took a few grams from one of the packets and gave it to me to sell. Then I went away. If there was one thing I really would have preferred not to do, it was this drug dealing. I'm not proud of it at all. Not because I would have got fifteen years if it hadn't been for the sentence reductions I earned by turning state's evidence, but because of the act of selling drugs itself. At least it's some consolation that the people I informed on who went to prison for drug dealing really deserved it. In the biggest trial I incriminated 112. More than a hundred people who wouldn't have been caught unless I'd exposed them. Anyway, my conscience is clear because I've never tried to hide the things I did myself.'

But all this self-sacrifice, hard work and soul-searching didn't really break up the network. Admittedly, there were a lot of arrests, but before long the whole system was up and running as effectively as ever, and the drugs were flowing in as easily as before. In 2009, three years after Di Bella's information had led to a major round-up, Lecco was again targeted by the law-enforcement agencies, and the District Anti-mafia Department, the Lecco Police and the Milan Guardia di Finanza netted some more of Coco Trovato's successors. One of the most important was 'The Banana', aka Vincenzo Falzetta, one of the boss's right-hand men, who had been sentenced to twelve years and six months but had been saved by a statute of limitations and was still at liberty.

According to the investigators' report, the boss's old lieutenant was arrested just as he was planning the strategy for the next phase of the clan's operations. The primary emphasis was on the building and earth-moving sectors, but the traditional business of drugs – mostly, ecstasy and cocaine – was not neglected. Nor were their investments in residential property – the 'Ndrangheta were expecting a boom after two years of stagnation – and the 'usual' commercial outlets: restaurants, bars, discotheques and pubs.

In Calolziocorte the new wave of arrests caught Giuseppe Elia, who had also been sentenced to twelve years at the end of Operation Oversize in 2006. Falzetta and Elia were important to the police – and to the clan – because they were also responsible for funding the upkeep of clan members who were in hiding and for the expenses of those who were in prison, notably Rodolfo 'The Gospel' Bubba. The nickname reflects the seventy-three-year-old's respected position in the clan. They trusted him for his wise counsel and always appealed to his authority before new members were baptized. It was Di Bella who had put him behind bars.

But even this latest round of arrests could not stop the 'Ndrangheta. And, in the end, one clan member, however senior, however respected, counts for little. What matters is not the individual, but the clan. It's almost Darwinian – the species has to be preserved and strengthened at all costs. After all, the stronger you are, the more profit you can generate. And for the 'Ndrangheta, profit is everything.

8

··

ARMS SMUGGLING

'Debt collection', to use Di Bella's ironic phrase for the work of the *pizzo* collector, drug dealing and murder were the stock in trade of the *'ndrine*. But there was another commodity no clan member could avoid – guns. The 'Ndrangheta needed a constant supply of arms, especially during 'duels' or clan wars between rival *'ndrine* to decide which clan was the strongest and which should get the largest slice of the proceeds. The only way to resolve such a dispute was with guns. It was years before the *'ndrine* succeeded in coming to a definitive agreement as to the size of the individual slices. In that time more than 700 people were killed among the clan members alone. But soon the clans' need to keep a well-stocked arsenal expanded far

··

beyond the need to eliminate their rivals. Gradually, the criminal arms race escalated until whole lorryloads of light, easy-to-use weapons were needed; they were used to kill rivals, but also to wipe out policemen who started asking tricky questions or to shoot a *carabiniere* in the face if he tried to intervene in a heist.

In the late 1980s and early 1990s guns had to be bought with cash, and Switzerland, the Middle East and the Balkans became three enormous shopping malls. Hand grenades bearing the red star of Tito's army and small Uzi machine-guns marked with the Star of David appeared in Lombardy and in southern Italy. When in 1993 eastern Europe began to produce the new Kalashnikov, the AK-74, ten million old AK-47s ended up in the Christmas sales. Not to mention the thousands of RPG-7s, Russian hand-held rocket-launchers. Cheap and old-fashioned enough to be frowned on by official armies and largely relegated to African guerrilla warfare, the RPG-7 lived out a happy retirement in the cavity walls of *picciottos'* houses. It didn't have the power to threaten a modern tank, but was perfectly adequate for knocking out a rival clan's 4×4, a magistrate's bullet-proof car or a security van on the *autostrada*.

To increase his arsenal, each boss set his labour force to work, sending his men out in search of weapons. Coco Trovato was no different from the others. The warring clans understood almost at once that, when peace was declared, that mass of weapons would make their owners' fortune. In the meantime, however, there was fighting to be done both in Reggio Calabria and in Milan. Some 'soldiers' fired; others went in search of munitions. 'Not everyone who works for the organization is the same. They have different interests, personal histories and characters. Each of them,' explains Di Bella, 'does best what comes easiest to him. If someone is good at laundering money, nobody asks him to pick up a pistol, draw up alongside a car at a traffic light and kill a person who needs to be punished. Because he'll make some mistake with the gun, and if that happens he won't be able to launder money either. It's a matter of team-work. But you never know the size of the team that has hired you. Whereas the person who hires you knows exactly what your role in the clan is.

'I never killed anyone – never have and never will. You need a special talent to do those things. Since that time when I witnessed the killing of Nino Castelnuovo's brother, I knew that each of us should follow his own road. Killing wasn't mine. Not that it bothered me to see someone die. Maybe that time was different, but usually if they kill you it's because you deserve it. It's the act itself that I find disturbing.

'You have to have a natural talent to be a killer, and I

don't have it. What I did was search for arms and sell them. I realized that the job suited me when I went to Switzerland for the first time in 1979. Until then I'd earned my living by collecting debts and doing other jobs for the clan. But now I suddenly found myself looking at huge profits – percentages with three zeros. So I did some sums and thought about how I could use my share and how I could reinvest it. I thought of two or three restaurants I could buy – one of them a beautiful place on the lakeside – the waiters I'd have to hire, the furniture I'd have to put in. I did have my fears. I was scared of being found out, not so much by the cops – the worst they could do would be to send me to prison for a while – but by my father. So whenever I went away for a few days I thought up some excuse. A different one every time. But there was no need that time. It was all over in a single day.'

•

'It was early in the summer of 1979. We drove to Zurich in two cars. I went with some friends. Agostino Rusconi (yes, him again), Sebastiano the Sardinian and some other members of Coco Trovato's gang. Rusconi was the most enthusiastic. It was he who persuaded me to go. He handled the contacts and made the rendezvous. We stopped at a big gun shop on the southern outskirts of Zurich. The owner was expecting us. He was of Italian origin and, from what they'd told me, had links to some of the money-changers at the casino in Campione as well as to some minor Swiss banks. And Coco Trovato, of course. We'd brought a suitcase of cash with us; it contained fifteen million lire. For that sum the gun dealer gave us forty pieces: 7.65 mm Beretta 70s and a few 38 mm Special revolvers. We put them in the boot of one of the cars, an Alfetta. There was room for everything, but only because we didn't buy any ammunition.

'We drove back to the border at Chiasso, stopping only once, for a meal. We had to reach customs while it was still daylight. Ten kilometres before the border, the Alfetta turned off towards Mendrisio. After Stabio, it turned onto an uphill track and went on climbing until the path petered out. There were four guys inside. Two of them got out. They put the guns in rucksacks, hoisted them onto their backs and crossed the pass along the smugglers' route. The other two returned to the main road and drove back to Lecco.

'In the meantime Agostino and I had gone on along the normal road to Chiasso. After we cleared customs we drove up into the hills above Como and then on to Bizzarone. We stopped in a small car park near a wood and waited for the two men who'd walked across the pass on foot to come out of the trees. Twenty minutes at most. When they arrived, they put their rucksacks in the boot, and we got back to Lecco just before nightfall. Two days later we handed over the forty guns to three Sicilian friends of Rusconi's in exchange for thirty million lire. They took them first to Reggio Calabria and then on to Palermo. We shared out the money equally and the next month we returned to Zurich. The following month we went three times. It became a regular routine. After our meetings the Swiss gun dealer reported the weapons stolen to the police and so got the insurance money too. It was a sure-fire scheme.

'So we decided to repeat the same operation in Valtellina. There were no clans there to run things. There was the local underworld, traditional smugglers of cigarettes, domestic appliances and alcohol. All the businesses revolving around Livigno, which was a tax haven. Coco Trovato often operated in the free-trade area and had some acquaintances among the smugglers. With all the bars and restaurants he ran, Franco was an excellent client, and what's more he had friends among the police, so he often sent empty lorries to Livigno, which returned full of alcohol and cigarettes. He sent tankers there too, which came back filled with heating oil. He made a profit on the kerosene, and so did the locals. So, in the early months of 1980, after

Franco had given the local mafias guarantees that we wouldn't be entering into direct competition with them, we started going round the valley. We started from Sondrio and visited the owners of almost all the gun shops in the province.

'In every village there was a contact, someone who was willing to visit the individual tradesmen on our behalf and propose the deal. Eighty per cent of them agreed. We'd arrive for our appointment and pay 300,000 lire for a Beretta worth 800,000. We'd take ten, the gun dealer would wait an hour and then call 113. By that time we'd be out of range of any roadblocks and he'd claim the money back on the insurance. If any dealer didn't cooperate or, worse still, tried to back out of the deal, so much the worse for him. We'd go ahead anyway – we'd rob him, frankly. We'd take the guns without paying and treat the dealer to a nice dose of arson. It was foolproof. And it made money for everyone. We went on like that for years – more than thirteen, in fact – especially for relatively small quantities. If we needed larger consignments we went to the usual Swiss suppliers or bought whatever was available on the market at the time.

'In November 1980 I started working as a security guard for ILVI – later renamed Sicuritalia. I got a gun licence and recruited some new colleagues who specialized in guns to Coco Trovato's gang. Three months after I was taken on, I heard that one ILVI employee was a former partisan from Mandello del Lario and had access to crates of guns, ammunition and hand grenades. I contacted him and offered him some money. He took us to a cave, in the mountains between Mandello and Abbadia Lariana. It was like a tunnel dug into the mountainside. We started from the church in Rongio, a little hamlet near Mandello, then walked uphill for about half an hour until we reached a track known locally as "the river path" because it runs alongside a stream. Then we went up the Alpe di Era to an altitude of almost 1,000 metres. We climbed even higher, then went downhill again, first across a meadow and then along a mule-track, until we came, several metres lower down, to the entrance of a huge cave. We walked past it and came to another cave, narrower and lower than the first. It contained the biggest cache of arms I'd ever seen: a lot of MG-42s, the heavy German machine-guns, dozens of boxes of 7.62mm bullets and even 80mm mortars. The ex-partisan had a small torch which didn't shed much light, but even so I could see wooden crates piled up one on top of the other, the specifications on them faded and covered with dust. Piles and piles of them.

'We made a note of the goods and walked downhill to an iron bridge, and soon afterwards we were back in Rongio, where we'd left the car. The next day I went to see the partisan again, this time with an envelope. It contained twenty million lire in cash, and I helped myself to two crates of guns, this time without taking the roundabout route as we had done the day before. It was a quick job, and a profitable one. The crates also contained four MG-42s, ideal for attacks on security vans. A week later I sold the whole lot for eighty million lire to three Sicilians who lived in Lecco. I think they sold them on in Brindisi. Since it was such a good deal, I couldn't keep it all to myself. If I had tried to and the clan had found out they'd have punished me. So I told Franco all about it as soon as I could.

'Before long we'd carried away practically the whole cache. But first I managed to do a little deal, again with the help of Rusconi. In between jobs, if the weather was fine, we used to go hiking in the mountains around Lecco. There was always a chance of stumbling across new business opportunities. A fortnight after the trek to reach the ex-partisan's cave, we happened to cross the Piani dei Resinelli, above Ballabio. Rusconi and I were with a small group of friends. When we got there, we found a dozen people firing small-bore revolvers. We were curious and we went over to them. We said straight away that we weren't cops, but they'd already figured that out for themselves. One of them was quite talkative. He said he was a secondary-school teacher in Bologna, but hailed originally from Caronia, near Messina. The very town where I was born. We started chatting about this and that, swapping news about the old folk of the village and discussing guns. Rusconi knew about the big partisan cache and he decided to chance his arm. He asked if they wanted to buy some higher-calibre guns, something with a bit more firepower. They accepted the offer, not least because the prices we quoted were very low. Thirty guns for five million lire. We sold them 9mm Berettas – a little out of date, but still very effective.

'The next day we went back to the Piani dei Resinelli. The group was still there training and before the transaction they told us in an undertone that they belonged to the Red Brigades. Maybe they'd made some inquiries about us before letting us in on the secret; at any rate they must have been certain that we weren't cops. We certainly didn't look like cops. Anyway, they stayed at Ballabio for no more than two weeks, then they disappeared. Rusconi reckoned they'd been arrested. But there was no way we were going to investigate. We didn't want to set off rumours. Asking questions wastes time and can get you into trouble. You might end up paying dearly for your curiosity. The secret is only to know about what really concerns you.

'On our many trips to Switzerland and our visits to the Valtellina to collect guns we'd got accustomed – I say we because we always did business in groups, or at least with a partner – to dealing with the same people every time. A few Sicilians who hung around Lecco or friends of the clan. We always had more or less the same clients. The faces might have changed, but the surnames didn't.

'In March 1990 there was a big round-up, both in northern Italy and in Calabria.[10] They confiscated hundreds of submachine-guns and pistols and thousands of rounds of ammunition and arrested about ten people. One of them was a bank clerk, and his arrest caused a sensation. I don't know why everyone was so surprised. Why shouldn't a man who wears a jacket and tie from Monday to Friday be a criminal on Saturday and Sunday? Anyway, the fuss soon died down, and two months later the stream of arms smugglers from Switzerland to Italy started flowing again. I don't have very clear memories of those years. I remember long car trips. Once from Lecco to Zurich, another time to Sondrio. Then Zurich again. But even if you stayed in one place, the organization brought you into contact with people of all races and weapons of all kinds.

'Once we even smuggled some uranium,' Di Bella went on. Judicial investigations into smuggling have revealed that uranium certainly was brought across the border between Italy and Switzerland in the early 1990s, hidden in a consignment of arms or in the boot of a car, in an attempt to evade customs controls. These were the years after the fall of the Berlin Wall when the conflict in the former Yugoslavia was at its height. Much of Europe was crawling with former KGB agents trying to boost their pension funds by selling arms or radioactive material from the former Soviet Union. Switzerland and the Balkans became the fishbowls that they swam about in.

There were plenty of fish; some were caught in police nets, others got through unscathed and at the end of the decade resumed careers as ostensibly reputable business-men. In Switzerland in 1991 Friedrich Leopold Renfer, honorary consul of Honduras and an alleged KGB agent, got into trouble with Swiss detectives. He was caught trying to transport nearly 30 kilograms of uranium to Serbia. He was aided in this enterprise by four Slavs and an Italian whom we can't name here, but who was later investigated by the Venetian judge Felice Casson on a charge of arms smuggling. It was a serious setback but not sufficient to put Leopold Renfer out of business. Two years later, in the summer of 1993, his name appears again in police files, this time in an account by a state witness, who described the monetary dealings of the Salvatore brothers, leading figures in Cosa Nostra. Renfer did their money launder-ing, and he also dealt in arms and uranium on behalf of the family. In fact, he had been doing so for some time.

Conceivably it had been the Salvatores who had, between 1979 and 1982, stood surety for the supply of uranium dioxide to the Iraqi dictator Saddam Hussein.

Renfer's operations extended much more widely than this, however. He didn't have an exclusive contract with a single family. From his consular office in Zurich he had for years been laundering money for the Morabitos, who along with the Palamaras and the Bruzzanitis were the most powerful clan in Lombardy. He did business with the Ferrara brothers, Calabrians now operating in Varese and the northern area of Milan. He was the consummate businessman, able to maintain relations with African dictators and former Soviet generals, buy arms from them, distribute the arms on the black market and, at the same time, steer them into legal channels to give the whole operation a semblance of respectability. After that he'd sell the weapons, through 'trusted' arms dealers and wholesalers, to the 'Ndrangheta. And yet at the same time he managed carefully to conceal any connection he had with the merchandise. The strings were pulled by middlemen working according to Renfer's general guidelines, and the 'dirty' work was entrusted to small-time smugglers from the Balkans.

'In the summer of 1993,' Di Bella recalls, 'I was contacted by an Albanian acquaintance of mine who operated in the area around Lake Como. He dealt in drugs, and he knew I dealt mainly in arms. He offered to act as an intermediary and to stand surety himself, so that he wouldn't have to reveal the names of the buyers. That was nothing out of the ordinary. I'd done business dozens of times with people I only knew by their first name. Often, even that name wasn't the one that appeared on their identity card either. It's a bad idea to ask questions. You're liable to end up the way a cop ends up when he sticks his nose in where he shouldn't. The person who stands surety is an important role in our line of work. And it's a well-paid one too. In those days you could earn as much as 10 per cent, and of large sums of money. In exchange the intermediary risks his reputation, and not only that. If the deal falls through, it's his job to intervene and plug the gaps. He can't get away with mere words. He has to pay the money out of his own pocket. If he doesn't have the money, he'll pay with a few days in a coma or even with his life.

'That summer I was offered the chance to sell 400 brand-new Skorpions, complete with their carrying cases, double clips, a cleaning kit and ammunition. 125 rounds each. The buyers were Croats. Naturally that was all I knew. The Albanian repeated that he would vouch for the buyers. My fear was that there was someone from Interpol trying to infiltrate us and stir things up. There was a war going on across the Adriatic, and every police force in Europe wanted to make an impression. To show the world that they could seal their borders and not let even one Beretta through. So the police were doing overtime on the road to and from Chiasso. However, since I knew the Albanian was reliable, I decided to accept. Through my contacts in Zurich I bought the material for about eighty million lire, and we arranged to meet at Brogeda, 100 metres from the railway station, just over the Italian border. I had Rusconi with me.

'There were five Croatians and they arrived dead on time in a white van with an Italian numberplate. It was probably stolen – in fact I'm sure it was. They parked. The driver remained at the wheel. The others got out. One pretended to go and buy some cigarettes and walked away. He was really covering his cronies' backs, and he made no effort to disguise the fact. Three of them came towards us. Only one spoke Italian, though badly. "You have all?" he asked. He was dressed in black. He was tall and muscular and had very short hair. I was tempted to ask, "You wouldn't by any chance be a soldier, would you?" I kept quiet. He was just another customer to us, after all, so we gave him the weapons, and that was that.

'They didn't even open any of the packages, and the one who seemed to be their leader repeated that we weren't to ask any questions. What kind of people did he think we were? We didn't even ask questions among ourselves, and

Rusconi was closer to me than a brother. We were hardly going to give a bunch of Croats the third degree. Agostino turned puce, but we decided to keep quiet. They were openly suspicious of us, and their leader and another guy kept us in Brogeda for about an hour. Long enough to give the others a head start if they were pursued. When the hour was up they made us a strange proposal: they offered us uranium in exchange for the guns. We barely even knew what uranium was, and we certainly had no idea what we could do with it. We replied that the agreement stipulated cash – paper money, and no tricks. We weren't in the habit of smuggling things that would be difficult to sell. It was tense for a while, and there was a bit of a stand-off. Then they took the money out of a dark-green plastic bag, and that was the end of the matter. They got into a car and waited for us to leave. We never met anyone from the Balkans again.'

•

Any gun shop can be a front for illegal trafficking. The continual movement of pistols and machine-guns from one country to another makes it easy for the 'Ndrangheta to play a gigantic three-card trick. The gun dealer himself, probably a perfectly ordinary businessman, a good husband and father, kids himself that he's a mere pawn, whereas in fact he too is a vital part of a criminal machine, though of course only the 'Ndrangheta have the complete picture and only the 'Ndrangheta hold the keys. The Zurich gun dealer and the criminal who smuggles the arms across the border don't know each another. The 'Ndrangheta, however, do: they know them both. They know all there is to know about both of them, and this enables them to fix the final price. Both of the guns and of the dealers' lives.

Di Bella's testimony is revealing: 'There was always an opportunity for doing business; even a relaxing evening out might turn into a job. In 1992 I met a woman called Francesca Fumagalli in Lecco. I'd been running bars for some time, and she was organizing the installation of the videopoker machines. One Friday I invited her to dinner the following evening. She said she was free and accepted my invitation. Over our third glass of wine we started talking about her activities abroad. She was quite well known at the time: she'd owned a firm which did a lot of business in France but it had gone bust, and she'd closed it down, leaving about a billion lire's worth of debts. In Italy, apparently, she had fewer contacts. I was more interested in her French dealings. At one point she told me she still went to France frequently – not on business these days, but to visit a friend – and added, "This friend of mine lives on a wonderful estate. Her father is a big arms manufacturer." She said this very knowingly, as if that was what she had been leading up to. The message was clear. So on our third meeting I asked her to introduce me to her friend. I met the friend not long afterwards at the Fumagallis' home in Molteno. I went with Agostino and a *brigadiere* in the prison service, Vincenzo Stoto. He was an arms expert and sometimes joined our group to do a bit of "overtime". He was basically a good man, poor guy. He came into contact with us because while working in prison he'd made friends with the brother of a member of the clan and had helped him with a job. Another time he'd gone to pick up some guns and gradually he'd gained the clan's trust.

'I was sorry to have to talk about him to the magistrates. But once you start to collaborate there's no going back. You inform even on people who've been close to you for years, people you've shared experiences with, at work or play. You have no alternative. It's like jumping off a bridge and not knowing how long it will be before you hit the ground. And without knowing whether they've tied a harness to you which might save your life. The only thing you can do is fall. And as you fall, you grab hold of anything, anyone that might help. You give them first names, surnames, you get people arrested. But nothing breaks your fall. Because you've signed an agreement and at the bottom of it, in very small print, there's a clause that says you've got to fall all the way down. Only then will you be a true *pentito*. I say this to explain why, even though Stoto always behaved well towards me, I didn't hide the fact that he was there too that evening in Molteno. Even though all he did was listen.

'Rusconi and I were very excited about the prospective deal and really went for it. We asked the French girl if it would be possible to order a lorryload of arms. We needed 7.65 mm pistols and especially Israeli-style submachine-guns. We had some Neapolitan friends who were interested in buying them. She agreed to supply the weapons, and didn't even seem particularly surprised. At that point I put the two parties in contact with each other, and the three of us left with a mediators' fee of about seventy million lire. The arms, Rusconi explained later, were sent from Nizza and travelled all the way along main roads, avoiding the *autostrada*, to Merone, in the province of Como. They went via Ventimiglia, where I'm sure the Frenchwoman had connections of some kind. Then, when they got near to Como, the lorry was handed over to the Neapolitans. And I don't know anything else, except that the operation was successful – very successful, in fact. But we never had any further contacts with the French, unfortunately. It's a pity not to keep a relationship like that going. To open a road that carries no risks, no costs and has a guaranteed profit, and then to see it all fade away . . . A pity. But the girl never came back to Italy, and you can't do that kind of business over the phone.'

In general the *'ndrine* make at least three billion euros a year from weapons,[11] with Lombardy, the Aosta Valley and Liguria the key points of transit. There are collusive gun dealers in the Valtellina and in Switzerland. Dealers in France are paid to import arms into Italy, while others in Liguria export weapons to France. But all the 'Ndrangheta's operations feed into one another. The money made from drugs is used to buy arms, and the profits from the sale of arms are then used to buy property – houses and even tourist facilities – semi-legitimate businesses, in fact, through which the money is very effectively laundered.[12] The processes are constantly refined but in essence they don't change. A recent case is worth describing.

In 2009 a father and son, the owners of the Calvini gunshop in the middle of Sanremo, were stopped on the Via Aurelia as they were approaching Bordighera – to be precise, as they were about turn into Strada Monte Nero, where Roberto Pellegrino lived. Pellegrino was a building contractor of Calabrian origin who had lived in Bordighera for many years. When the lower-ranking of the two policemen looked in the boot, he found a pistol and a rifle, which didn't tally with the documents the dealers were carrying. The two men were arrested. At the trial they defended themselves by saying that it was a minor administrative error and that the guns were for a client they believed to be French, although he was in fact an Italian wanting to smuggle arms abroad. The judge did not believe their defence; nor did he believe that they had acted in good faith. He sentenced father and son to two years and four months' imprisonment each. Pellegrino, the entrepreneur, got two years. However, the case has gone to appeal, so it will be some time before the Calvini file can be declared finally closed.

•

The illegal arms trade takes us on a long journey, from one end of Italy to another and deep into the mysteries of the First Republic.

Twenty years ago Giuseppe Di Bella was involved in one of the most tragic episodes in the history of modern Italy, an incident which would prove to be a political turning point. The 'Ndrangheta and the mafia work together, though their reciprocal agreements are not always a success. 'Often,' says Di Bella, 'the alliances you find yourself making in order to conclude a deal are temporary or the result of chance encounters. And besides, you mustn't imagine that everything inside the 'Ndrangheta is rigid and decided from above. Everyone has some scope for free enterprise, whether they're members or friends. Of course, you mustn't interfere with anyone else's interests. Also, if you earn a hundred, you automatically have to pay forty to those who protect you. If you respect these two basic rules, you can make a living. In fact, to be honest, you can make a very good living. So I did some things entirely on my own initiative. For example, in June 1992, thanks to the mediation of a Sicilian friend who was much older than me, I went on a long journey to sell arms in Sferracavallo, north of Palermo, near Isola delle Femmine. My contact there told me that an acquaintance of his was looking for someone who could get him some brand-new, unused Beretta pistols and Skorpion submachine-guns. That someone was Nino 'u Sfregiatu, 'Scarface'. All I knew about him was that he had been involved in the assassination of Giovanni Falcone just outside Capaci that May.'

Scarface's real name was Antonino Gioè, and he was a trusted aide of Giovanni Brusca, the prime mover in the operation. The two men acquired the explosive for the bomb together. Gioè waited for Falcone's armour-plated cars and made a call on his mobile phone when he saw them leave the airport and notified someone close to Brusca, whereupon Brusca himself pressed the button. Gioè liked to be called Nino, and he liked to talk about the things he'd done, to boast about his friendships and the powerful circles that he moved in. He used the phone a lot, and that made it easier to arrest him and earned him a new nickname, 'u Chiacchierone, 'the blabber'. All his talking on the phone cost him a prison sentence, and later, perhaps, his life. He'd said too much about the *attentatuni* – the Sicilian term for the Capaci bomb attack – and mentioned the key names of Nitto Santapaola and Giuseppe Pulvirenti. He also made unguarded references to a TNT attack on the Palermo law courts and the execution of twelve officers of the prison service on duty in Pianosa. Worst of all, he liked joking, and didn't hold back when talking about his boss. He said one of those things that the code doesn't forgive: 'Who the hell does this Bagarella think he is? Only joking.' The butt of the joke was not amused. So in June 1993 Gioè committed suicide in his cell, or somebody gave him a helping hand, because as well as his loose tongue he had made too many unforgivable mistakes, such as making friends with Paolo Bellini, the extreme rightwinger with links to the secret services, one of the planners of the series of mafia attacks on art galleries and historic churches in the spring and summer of 1993.

Di Bella continues his story. 'I was working as a barman at the time, so I took a week's holiday to go to Sicily. I left Lecco on Tuesday morning at dawn and sixteen hours later

I arrived in Sferracavallo. The next day, in the early afternoon, I went to the local billiard hall, where Nino was
waiting for me. He was young, tall. He was definitely under
forty and he had a mark on his left cheek, like a faint scar.
The clock showed two in the afternoon. In Sicily, unlike in
Milan, there's no point in getting up early. Unless they have
to kill someone, the mafiosi always get up late. At one or
two in the afternoon. Then they go from bar to bar to drink
coffee and, more importantly, to be seen. You can only contact them after that. There's no point in looking for them
any earlier. It's a matter of form. And if you go to Palermo,
you need to know these things. You also have to know that
if you come straight to the point you'll make the person
you're dealing with suspicious. First you have to talk about
Sicily, about the flavours and colours of the island. Only
then do you pull out your ace.

'That's what I did with Nino; in fact we didn't talk about
real work for more than ten minutes – not until Giovanni
Brusca came into the bar. The two men knew each other
well; they greeted each other affectionately and embraced. I
was introduced to Brusca. He asked about me. Quite rightly,
he wanted to know why I was there and what references
I had. I replied in the proper way and added that when I
looked at him it was as if I was looking at the twin of a man
from my own village. He bore a striking resemblance to a

friend of mine from Caronia. Brusca commented that it was a blessing to have a common kind of face, because it brought only advantages.

'Later, when the conversation returned to the subject of arms, I addressed Brusca directly and offered to sell him some explosives and some gunpowder. I told him I could get it from Switzerland at competitive prices. "We have large amounts of explosive only a stone's throw from here and we can get it without running any risks," Brusca said, with a smile on his lips. Then he went out and made a gesture to the barman with his left hand, as if to say, "everything's under control".

'We left the billiard hall as well and went to eat bread and *panelle*. I continued to talk about the explosives. I'd gone all that way, so it would have been useful to sell some. But Nino just repeated what Brusca had said, "We have some reliable people working in the powder magazine at Isola delle Femmine. Whenever we need anything, all we have to do is knock at the side gate." He ended by saying that the explosive for the Capaci bomb had come from that source and that soon more of it would be used "to make a big bang".'

Just outside Isola delle Femmine there's a little gully. It starts by the sea, passes under the *autostrada* which links the airport to Palermo and climbs up through a dense wood. All the other green areas around the Sicilian capital have been obliterated by cement; the woodland of Isola delle Femmine is unique in that it has not. It is 450,000 square metres in size, and the gully is effectively hidden by it. Halfway up, towards the top, you see a soldier looking out from a watchtower which seems to be perched on the tunnel of the *autostrada*. He is heavily armed. On the other side of the barbed wire is a huge munitions depot. It is run by the Italian Navy but is in fact chiefly used by NATO. Two or three times a year foreign ships arrive in the little harbour below and unload crate after crate. Occasionally a military helicopter lands in the dense woodland and takes off again soon afterwards.

In the middle of the base is a large heliport that can be reached via a steep road carved out of the rock. Along the road some tunnels have been dug into the mountainside: six in all; the shortest is 650 metres long, the longest 950 metres. A gate bars the entrance to tunnel number one – the one with the NATO symbol. There are all manner of strange stories and rumours attached to these tunnels: that nuclear warheads are stored in them, or that top-secret experiments are carried out there. This veil of mystery suits the mafia down to the ground. A parliamentary question was once tabled concerning the tunnels,[13] but it didn't shed much light. As it happens, the truth is less mysterious than it seems, though far more chilling. The tunnels are packed with munitions – large-calibre guns and missiles. More importantly, though, the mountain also contains enough gelignite to blow it apart.

In 1992 the gully was properly maintained. In fact, it was so clear that you could walk along it without the slightest difficulty. So it was easy to carry the explosive from the base to the *autostrada* along the strip of cement and then place it under a layer of asphalt a short distance from the mouth of the gully, the same asphalt that blew up on 23 May 1992, taking Giovanni Falcone, his wife and their three bodyguards with it.

'After Nino mentioned the bombing I changed the subject,' Di Bella goes on. 'In fact, for a few seconds my instinct told me to walk away. After all, the only thing I was interested in was what I had travelled sixteen hours by car for: selling arms. All this mafia plotting wasn't for me. But he insisted that we spend the afternoon together, so I couldn't say no. We went to several bars in Sferracavallo, Tommaso Natale and Isola delle Femmine – the whole western coast of Palermo. We talked some more about arms, about Switzerland and about how easy it was for us to cross the border and get stuff.

'At about four o'clock, since he'd returned to the subject, I asked him if I could meet Brusca again. I was desperate to make some kind of deal with him, even though I knew it was risky. Those guys are utterly ruthless. Friendship doesn't come into it. Only two things matter to them: business and death. Franco would have forgiven me a mistake made in good faith. They wouldn't. With those mafiosi, one day you're useful and everything's fine, the next day you're an inconvenience and, without even telling you, they put you in their little black book. And as soon as they get the chance, they kill you.

'But I really wanted to return to Lecco in triumph. If I could strike a bargain with Brusca, it would be a feather in my cap. I don't know if Nino understood what was going through my head, but we took a boat from the harbour of Isola delle Femmine and in a few minutes we arrived at a yacht. He was taking me to see Giovanni Brusca again. The yacht was an incredible size. I've never seen one so big. I didn't see its name or its registration number. But I didn't ask any questions. We climbed on board, then took off our shoes. Nino opened a sliding door which led first to a sort of ante-room, then along a corridor to a lounge.

'There, sitting in an armchair, was the Christian Democrat politician, life senator and former prime minister, Giulio Andreotti. Beside him, and facing Brusca, was the former President of the Republic, Giovanni Leone. There were some other people standing up who I didn't know.

Distinguished-looking people. There was one man who looked like Amedeo Nazzari, the actor. I remember him well because his face was the first one I saw when Nino opened the door. Just before my eyes met Andreotti's. "Hey," I said to Nino, "isn't that the Hunchback [one of Andreotti's nicknames]? What's he doing here?"

'"What do you think he's doing?" he replied in Sicilian. "He comes here and he gives orders."

'"Gives orders?" I said to myself. But no words came out of my mouth, and Nino kept quiet as well.

'I made a gesture with my head to Nino. He must have calculated on getting me a meeting with Brusca alone to talk about arms and he seemed as surprised as I was to find those men there. I followed him, and we went out again. Neither of us talked. Ten minutes had passed in all. There were too many important people there, and I wanted to leave. So I put on my shoes and said, "Nino, let's go." I'd realized there was something wrong. I have a feel for these things. "Maybe I'll come down some other time. We'll talk about it later – I can see Brusca's busy. Thanks for your help, but I'd like to go back now."

'So we got back into our boat and ten minutes later we were already at Isola delle Femmine. We moored at a point close to a level crossing. We crossed the road and went into a bar-patisserie to drink a glass of water and eat a *cannolo*.

I've always had a bad habit of getting up and going to pay. I did so on that occasion too, but the lady behind the counter looked at me in horror: "Are you joking? You'll get me into trouble." Indeed, in all the time I'd been with Scarface I'd never seen him pay. That was his kingdom; it belonged to him and to other mafiosi like him. Everybody knew them, because they did everything quite openly.

'If you own even the people, there's no reason why you shouldn't meet a prime minister in broad daylight. I didn't care. It wasn't my business to speculate about what Andreotti was doing with Brusca. At any rate, after the *cannoli* my relationship with Nino cooled: we parted on the understanding that I'd get in touch again a month later through our mutual friend and supply him with fifty Skorpions. But in the event the deal didn't work out, and I didn't go back to Sicily for several years. About three months after that meeting, Paolo Borsellino [the anti-mafia judge] was killed in Palermo. When I heard about it on the news I was a bit scared, because it was exactly what Nino had said would happen. Another "big bang". I knew too much for my own liking. It didn't suit me. I was interested in making money and doing business. When it came to shady dealings involving the authorities I wasn't happy at all.'

Di Bella takes a deep breath. He stops and looks at us.

He has told the whole story of his Sicilian journey without stopping, as if to unburden himself of something that he has kept buried for years. We too take a deep breath. What he has told us is very different from what we had always understood to be the case. We had thought that the various criminal organizations were quite distinct. Now we had to face up to the fact that there are no borders between the mafias. There is no separation between the Camorra, the mafia and the 'Ndrangheta. It's one single fabric. It's the same disease, the same cancer spreading throughout the body of the state. Their terrifying power lies precisely in their ability to be flexible and fluid, to interact with one another, to share business opportunities. Their web spreads right across Italy – and beyond. And all any of us can do is to try to expose it for what it is and share everything Di Bella has told us with the anti-mafia authorities. It is for them to assess his startling testimony and, if they think fit, to conduct new investigations in the hope that another branch of the criminal network can be cut down.

EPILOGUE

Pippo Di Bella should be happy. After ten years as a *pentito*, hidden from sight on a witness protection programme, the invisible man has at last returned to real life: a new home, the search for a job, the chance to build relationships and emotional ties, an identity, after the long and exhausting journey he travelled as a man of the 'Ndrangheta. But he's not happy; he's afraid.

Di Bella lives in Lombardy, in a rented flat measuring just 40 square metres, with only one bedroom and a double bed he has to share with his eleven-year-old son, who is a picture of silent despair. The windows look onto the street. The television is always on, his bank balance always in the red.

'When I moved to this village, in an area of Lombardy that the Trovatos didn't control, I thought I would never meet any of my former associates again. Ten years had passed; I thought I was free to start work, to build myself a future, but I was wrong. One morning I was walking along the street when I passed one of Franco's men, a guy who worked for his brother Mario. It only took a glance, a meeting of the eyes, for me to know. He pretended not to recognize me but it was clear that he'd understood only too well who I was: he slowed down and stiffened.

'If I've met one of them here, it means the Trovatos' influence is everywhere now. They've started up again, and they're even more dangerous than before. Lately I've been asking around, trying to find out what they're doing. I've talked to friends and found out that the Trovatos have already opened six or seven new bars or restaurants. They're powerful, they can do what they like, and under Mario's leadership they're frightening. Mario came out of prison after years in solitary. His driving licence has been cancelled and he's not allowed to run any kind of club or restaurant. But he opens them anyway by registering them in the name of some front man, and if you go into one of them you're quite likely to find him inside, dressed in jacket and tie. He's the boss. The *carabinieri*, the police, everyone knows what's going on, but he still gets licences through people who work for the regional council or the chamber of commerce, people Franco has always kept on his side. If Mario Trovato met me he could easily cut my throat in the street – he's too impulsive to play it cool, and he doesn't give a damn about going to jail. Such indifference to prison is very common among the *'ndrine*. Prison isn't seen as a place of punishment; on the contrary, being in there is a matter of pride.

'Mario has taken over the running of the organization, and his right-hand man is a supposedly reliable state witness, Omega [the code name of a person who may be the subject of new investigations]. After the police round-ups of the 1990s there was a slump; things became disorganized. There were too many operations in progress, and the Sirianni group, which had recently become the executive arm of the clan, couldn't handle them all. So Franco ordered Omega, who was already a well-known figure, to pretend to turn state's evidence. He agreed and began to collaborate with the authorities. Omega led a double life for a few years. He did the usual things a state witness does, though he was risking his life, because there were plenty of people who didn't know what was really going on and had it in for him: "We'll kill him when he comes out," they used to say.

'I was out of prison at the time and I found out that Omega had turned *pentito* on Franco's orders. I met him one day and I asked him what the hell he thought he was doing. He said, "Go away, I'm under escort." A few weeks later I saw him again, near Lake Como. He was doing some work with mechanical diggers – pretending to be a labourer when he was really the boss: all the firms there worked for Franco. Again I asked him what he was up to. He said, "Don't worry, I had to turn *pentito*, but it's all a sham. I have to save the organization. If I don't do this, the whole thing is going to collapse." I said, "You'd better watch out, there a lot of people gunning for you." He wasn't in the least concerned: "What do I care? I've got an escort and I can go wherever I like." That was true enough: he did have an escort that went around with him everywhere, and he was certainly well protected. Later, when word got around that he'd turned *pentito* for the sake of the organization, the fuss died down, and he wasn't harmed. Soon, he began dealing in videogames, construction firms and estate agencies. He took control of everything, with the help of the money he got from the state for his "cooperation". Now Mario's out too, and the whole business is starting up again in a big way. The 'Ndrangheta are growing so strong it's frightening. Anything they can't run themselves they contract out to the Chinese, just like before. They don't miss a trick.'

As we talk, Di Bella constantly looks around the apartment, checking all the time. The building is vulnerable to attack. It has no porter's lodge, the front gate is often left open, the hall is dark. In fact, everything that goes on in the flat is clearly visible from the neighbouring buildings. He decides we should go down to the garage where he parks his car, which is under the railway station. There's nobody there; trains make an infernal noise when they pass by. It's the perfect place for an ambush, and we're beginning to feel uneasy ourselves.

'Now they know where I live. They start with with some simple tests. The other night someone buzzed at the entry-phone at five in the morning. I didn't answer, because I knew perfectly well what they were after. They want to make you look out of the window, or maybe trick you into going downstairs with some excuse, then shoot you with a pistol. I know the method – the men may change, but the organization and its modus operandi never do. I used the same trick myself in my day: a buzz at the door, and the guy sticks his head out of the window to see who the hell it is. I've seen all their tricks before and done them myself, so I'm not going to fall for them. I know they'll get to me sooner or later, but it's up to me to defend myself, seeing that the law won't do it. There are too many things I know about them.

'For example, there are some other unsolved murders where I know the identity of the killer and the person who hired him, and his motive. Like the murders committed during attacks on security vans. The usual method was to make a deal with an inside man, one of the security guards, before you carried out the heist. He had to delay giving the alarm, and in return he'd get a third of the takings: "We'll rob you, then we'll drive off into the mountains or somewhere else with the van. You wait twenty minutes, then raise the alarm." Sometimes, though, the boys couldn't make a deal with the guards, and if that happened, they'd kill them. Maybe not straight away – they might wait months, so that the two events seemed unconnected. Omega killed two security guards, but was never implicated in the investigations. The widows must still be in mourning.

'I have to watch out for these signs, but I can't let my son see what I'm doing. I mustn't show any hesitation, because I'm all he's got. He's already afraid of going to school. To get there he has to walk along the road beside the railway. A few years ago a sixteen-year-old girl was snatched on that same stretch of road and then killed. On the news they said the murderer was crazy, that it was an act of madness; but we knew the family. My son is scared the same thing will happen to him. Now and then he asks me, "Papa, what if they shoot us?" I'm all he's got. Most people can count on uncles, cousins, brothers; my son has got no one now. His mother's gone, and his uncles are members of the 'Ndrangheta.'

Giuseppe Di Bella has lost his relatives. Some disown him, others cold-shoulder him. The most telling example is that of his brother Rosario, who joined the organization after Pippo's arrest: 'Now he's in the organization, he's chauffeur to Mario, Franco's brother. He registers bars and restaurants in his name, he's bought a luxury flat and a flashy car. He's bought a car for his son too, and another for his wife, who goes out to lunch with Mario's lover. But sooner or later they'll kill him, because they won't think he's a hundred per cent reliable. When he came to the trial in the high-security courtroom he publicly insulted me as he walked past. He shook hands with all the criminals in the court, but he gave me a look of contempt. He was trying to dissociate himself from me. What he doesn't realize is that it'll count against him.

'I know how they think, and the kind of thing they say: I may be a self-confessed traitor, but at least I've been open about accusing them in court. But my brother first disowns me and then goes to work with them. I know the organization will be asking themselves: which of the brothers is more trustworthy: Pippo or Rosario? They won't be sure. They're using him as their handyman at the moment, but they'll soon begin to wonder how far they can trust someone who disowns his own brother and sides with them. Clan members never disown each other, they've always stuck together.

'When my wife died, my brother said he was sorry but

he didn't want anything more to do with me. Our relatives were forced to choose between him and me. So he's doubly a traitor; sooner or later they'll get rid of him. I can already imagine how they'll do it: they'll set him up. He drives Mario's car for him, because Mario hasn't got a licence. One day the boss will tell someone to ambush them. They'll kill my brother, then they'll spread a rumour that it was a way of getting back at me, an insult to my family. They'll kill him, I can guarantee it.

'And yet he could easily have remained in the clan without disowning me. All he'd have had to say was, "Listen, boys, I'm my own man. I'm not like my brother. My brother's the traitor. If you want me to stay, I'll stay. I'll even change my surname; or if you don't want me around, I'll leave. But I'll never disown my brother; my mother is his mother." That way they'd have respected him; but he thought he knew better than anyone else. He should know how they think – he's grown up with them. And yet, for all his intelligence, he made the mistake of abandoning me for them. He was a good barman, but he wasn't satisfied with that. Now I hope in my heart that he gets arrested sooner or later, because that's the only way he might perhaps avoid being killed.'

•

'When my wife died I had first-hand experience of how the authorities can hurt you. It's different from the way the 'Ndrangheta hurts you. She fell ill in February 2009 and died on 22 July of the same year. When we found out about her illness I took her to a clinic in Peschiera del Garda, and the doctors told me she had six months to live. It was my fault she'd got cancer: it was the stress of constantly moving from one town to another. But you know about that part of my life. My first thought, when the doctors read out their notes, was that perhaps she could live longer than they had predicted. So I immediately asked to speak to Luca Masini, the public prosecutor, who was responsible for my protection. Masini wasn't interested, he just wouldn't listen. I contacted him so many times I lost count. But it was no good. The last time I spoke to him was when I got the De Pascalis brothers arrested – two criminals from Lecco that he was particularly interested in. I left a message on his voicemail telling him that my wife was dying and that I wanted to take her to another clinic to see if there was anything they could do for her. He didn't reply.

'Federica was getting worse and worse, and he informed me, through the secretariat, that I'd have to make a written application if I wanted to speak to him. It was incredible! Whenever he needed me to testify or to answer some questions he'd come round to my flat at four o'clock in the morning, and nobody made any written requests then. I know everyone has to do his own job, but do you stand on formality when a woman's dying? But that's what happened: whenever he needed something, I'd have to go straight off to testify in case the remand period expired and the man they'd arrested had to be released. He was happy enough to see me at times like that – he'd come round to pick me up at once. But when I was in need, he let me down.

'My wife died in July. I called him again because I didn't know where to bury her. By the terms of the law she had to be buried in the cemetery in Florence, since she was registered as a resident there. But her parents couldn't go to Tuscany to mourn her. I rang Galileo Proietto, the other public prosecutor I worked with. He understood the problem. I think he did something – he must have got on the phone to someone, because eventually the town council of Lecco agreed to let my Federica be buried there. Whenever I think about it I feel immense gratitude to Proietto as a man and as an investigator. But he's unique.

'Many state witnesses are more direct than me and negotiate over the evidence they give. They say, "I'm not talking unless you put all my family under protection, including my cousins." They know very well that no one would ever touch those relatives, because anyone who works in the 'Ndrangheta knows what to expect. So a *pentito* will ask for protection for three or four times the number of people who really need protecting, because of that maintenance cheque that arrives at the end of the month. The more people there are, the richer he is. But it's stolen money. I'm surprised that the authorities agree to throw away so much money. There are a lot of families who make a living out of this system. There are just under 1,000 *pentiti*. But if you include all the cousins, great-grandchildren and other relatives being supported by the state, the actual total is 11,000 people. So there are 10,000 relatives, and three-quarters of them are scroungers. If I were in charge I'd reform the whole system. In the first place, the law states that you must talk in the first 180 days of the protection programme: it would be better to extend the period to leave more time for the investigations. And then, when the court cases are over, the programme ought to stop too. I don't see why a person should remain under protection for ten years, or indefinitely. Secondly, people under protection usually don't work. The paperwork makes it too complicated, so you end up living like a vegetable, doing nothing. You feel embarrassed in front of your family because you don't have a job. Your son can see it in your eyes. But you can't escape from the vicious circle you've got yourself into.

'Then one day you get the message you've been waiting for all these years. Your lawyer calls you on your mobile to say that the contract you signed with the authorities will expire in three months' time. That's the word he uses: "expire". It's a nasty word because when you hear it you start wondering, "What am I going to do now?" You make inquiries and discover that during the years you've been under protection you haven't made any contributions towards your pension. Of course you haven't: you don't exist. The documents you receive show a fictitious address. All the *pentiti* and relatives under escort are registered as living in the same *carabinieri* barracks. I've never even been there. But being registered there means that you can't take decisions for yourself. If you want to find a regular job, a place where everyone will accept you, the application has to be made through the central office; and it takes months for anything to happen.'

•

'They'll get me in the end. The 'Ndrangheta's reasoning is simple: if a guy needs to be killed quickly because he's a threat to some job they're planning, he'll be dead before the day is out; but if he's committed an offence against the organization – and I've committed the most serious one in the book – they'll wait until things have cooled down. Then one fine day you'll be sitting quietly at a table in a restaurant, or maybe at the wheel of your car, lighting a cigarette. Several years will have gone by and you'll have forgotten all about it. You won't be thinking you have to die. That's when they'll kill you. It might take one year, it might take two or three. It might even take as long as ten years, because the 'Ndrangheta are quite happy to let a decade pass if they have to. Then someone will come knocking at your door.'

Today, Di Bella is still afraid of death – his own and that of those closest to him. He's also worried that the publication of this book will force him back into a protection programme; since it came out he has been living in a secret location, with a mobile security guard provided by the *carabinieri*, while the investigations into his statements continue. He is haunted by memories and by the thought of all those people who can't forgive him for testifying against an organization whose power is constantly growing.

According to the research institute Eurispes (2008 data) the 'Ndrangheta clans have a turnover of more than 44 billion euros a year, equivalent to 2.9 per cent of Italy's GDP. They constitute a cartel in the semi-monopoly that is the European cocaine trade: 62 per cent of their turnover comes from drug smuggling, with 400,000 kilos imported every year at a 400 per cent profit on the Colombian raw material.

The 'Ndrangheta has modified its organization, adapting its structure to the needs of expansion and leadership. The most recent investigations by the public prosecutors Ilda Boccassini and Nicola Gratteri, in Milan and Reggio Calabria respectively, reveal a pyramidal structure similar to that of Cosa Nostra: at the apex is an advisory body, the so-called *crimine* ('crime'), which provides a link to covert masonic lodges, crucial to the organization's self-preservation and consolidation. Next we have the *società maggiore* of the bosses, then the three *mandamenti* ('districts') of Calabria, and on down to the *locale*, made up of all the *'ndrine* in any one area. There are seventy-three clans in Reggio Calabria alone.

The economic crisis in Europe is accelerating the spread of organized crime in Portugal, Spain, Germany and, of course, Italy. The recession, and the stagnant economy, have ensured that the 'Ndrangheta become even stronger, their supermarket trolley piled high with bankrupt businesses, answerable to no one. Faced with this scenario, the Italian government just dithers. And so does the rest of Europe. Populist solutions like sending the army to Calabria are of no avail. The drug smugglers are protected by *omertà*, not just on the plain of Gioia Tauro but also in wealthy Brianza, in the Italian community of Dortmund in Germany, a centre for money-laundering, and in Hamburg, where the authorities admit that they can only stop a tiny percentage of the cocaine that passes through the city's docks.

The EU has yet to understand that defeating the 'Ndrangheta should be a top priority. It needs to attack them on all fronts – financial, judicial, political, cultural and even military. Until that happens, the cancer of crime will spread inexorably. After all, the criminals are not so very different from us. More and more people enter the organization not by choice but out of need, the need for money, for security, for work. They are subjugated by a stark threat: 'Work with us or die.'

The 'Ndrangheta is the most shadowy of the international criminal organizations. More than half the murders of its members remain unsolved. Many are not even attributed to mafia bullets, because these cases, whether in northern Italy or in Germany, are often not classified as mafia crimes but are filed with ordinary crimes and quickly forgotten. They are dismissed in newspaper reports as generalized 'revenge attacks' or seemingly motiveless killings because often the victim has no criminal record. He had an impeccable cover: builder, bank clerk, lawyer, neighbour. And in dismissing these crimes, yet another opportunity for exposing what is really happening is lost. Apparently, no one sees the extent to which ordinary society has been penetrated by organized crime, nor the clans' almost military hold over their territories, whether in Italy, in Germany or in Spain, nor their colonization of Canada, the United States and Australia.

The 'Ndrangheta's roots in Calabria, in Locride and in Aspromonte – poverty-stricken areas seemingly without influence – protect it. It seems to be under the radar, rural, poor – why would the authorities bother? And the fact that blood ties hold the clans together means that any betrayal of the clan is almost unthinkable, and this strengthens the organization still further. The *'ndrine* stick together – at all costs. The chance of any clan member turning state's evidence is remote. The ratio of state witnesses is almost one to a hundred compared to Cosa Nostra: you have to wait for a hundred Sicilian *pentiti* before you'll find one from the 'Ndrangheta.

But then the 'Ndrangheta has always been underestimated, always considered to be less important than Cosa Nostra and the Camorra, both in Italy and in the rest of the world. But it is an organization with a terrifying reach and it exerts a vicious hold on Italy and, indeed, the rest of Europe

Giuseppe Di Bella and Filippo Barreca have staked everything on making the giant leap from clan member to state witness. But they are far from convinced that their decision has brought about any significant changes. And it is a sad truth that the reminiscences of former members alone will never be enough to bring down the clans. At least not until we all understand that there is a war on, a war being waged by the 'Ndrangheta against us all.

Acknowledgements

We are grateful to the magistrates Giancarlo Capaldo and Nicola Gratteri, and Deputy Public Prosecutor Galileo Proietto of the District Anti-mafia Office of Milan, for their help.

We would also like to thank Maurizio Belpietro and Ferruccio de Bortoli, without whose advice this book would not have been published.

Our thanks are also due to Giuseppe Di Bella and Filippo Barreca for their courage in coming forward with their information; to investigators such as Giovanni Capello; to Barbara Reggiani for her meticulous work in transcribing the recordings; and to all the other people who have contributed to the publication of this book and who for various reasons cannot be named.

Lastly, we would like to thank Camilla and Valentina for their trust and patience.

Endnotes

∙∙∙

1. There have been dozens of investigations into the criminal organizations of northern Italy, and every year the public prosecutors of Lombardy and the neighbouring regions continue to bring charges and convict numerous criminals, forcing the clans to keep changing and making new alliances. The following are the main Lombard investigations into the 'Ndrangheta and allied groups.

Operation Wall Street. Launched in 1991 and coordinated by the public prosecutor Armando Spataro, the inquiry took its name from the pizzeria headquarters of Coco Trovato and, in its Lombard branch alone, revealed the involvement of the 'Ndrangheta in of all kinds of activity along the Lecco–Milan axis and throughout Brianza. 139 people were remanded in custody; huge estates were seized, including 16 businesses (gyms, pizzerias, shops and estate agencies); 20 properties (villas, flats and land) were confiscated, along with 60 current and deposit accounts and 50 high-powered cars.

∙∙∙

Operation Countdown. This followed the previous operation and completed the map of relations between the Lombard mafias, sending a number of bosses and ordinary criminals to jail. It also investigated the murder of Roberto Cutolo, son of Raffaele.

Operation Final Act. In 2002 Deputy Public Prosecutors Alberto Nobili and Marco Alma examined the details of numerous murders carried out in the preceding years, starting with the extermination of the Batti family by the Flachi–Coco Trovato axis. Their reconstruction confirmed the links between the various mafias. The picture that emerged from it was that of a *pax mafiosa* punctuated with murders.

Operation North-South. 221 people, both Calabrians and Sicilians, were remanded in custody: this inquiry made it possible to reconstruct two decades of criminal activity in Milan and several neighbouring towns, mainly to the south of the city. The offices of three lawyers were raided, and a general of the *carabinieri* was issued with formal notice that he was under investigation. This inquiry revealed the background to 9 kidnappings, 14 murders, 40 robberies and some huge consignments of drugs. The complex charges included a case of money laundering through Switzerland.

Operation Milan Car Park. This operation was carried out on the initiative of the Anti-mafia Department of Florence, which, following other trails, arrived at Milan Car Park, an exchange market of arms and drugs between the north, centre and south of Italy, run by Sicilians connected with the Cursoti group. The freemasons were also caught up in the inquiry.

Operation Duomo Connection. Starting in 1988 from some phone-taps and tailing of suspects by the *carabinieri*, the investigation initially revealed a drug-smuggling operation run jointly by Sicilians and Calabrians, and later led to the discovery of collusion between mafiosi and some members of Milan City Council, the aim of which was to make a political carve-up worth billions of lire. This investigation was in fact the precursor of Tangentopoli, or 'Bribesville'.

Operation Gelmini. The inquiry carried out along the Gela–Milan axis brought to light the links between the mafia gangs of the two cities: the structure of the organization, the people involved, the modes of communication and the businesses run in the north by the Gela clans.

Operation Murcia. In various provinces of Lombardy, and in Spain, the *carabinieri* of the Special Operations Taskforce, together with local units and the Spanish police, arrested people considered responsible for criminal association for the purpose of international drug smuggling.

Operation The King. This investigation, which began in December 2004 after the seizure of 22 kilos of cocaine in a Milan flat, led to the discovery of a high-level international crime network run by the Calabrian Morabito-Palamara clan, which imported large amounts of drugs into the Lombard capital and invested and laundered the proceeds of the drug trade in a network of companies and workers' and transport cooperatives in the wholesale markets of Milan. Eleven firms were raided, all of which centred on the fruit and vegetable market in Via Lombroso. They included Sogemi, the firm wholly owned by Milan City Council which ran the wholesale markets. The nightclub 'For a King' was placed under distraint, and 250 kilograms of cocaine were seized. Among the seventy people investigated were an officer of the local police who worked in the food section (the department responsible for the control of shops and restaurants) and some employees of the licensing departments of two Lombard councils.

2. Concerning Perego Costruzioni, the investigating magistrate Giuseppe Gennari writes in his warrant for the application of precautionary measures requested by the public prosecutor Ilda Boccassini: 'Here we have some gentlemen, lacking any professional qualification which might justify their attitude, claiming the right to decide who is to administer a certain company, who is to be dismissed, who must give up his post to whom and how the jobs are to be assigned; and doing this while constantly shuttling back and forth between Lombardy and distant Calabrian localities where other gentlemen – resident in San Luca and Rosarno – are called upon to

settle controversies with an authority that is recognized without debate and without doubt by all concerned. Now, according to normal logic all this is senseless, and it confirms Calabrian organized crime's astonishing capacity for control and its level of internal structuring, if the phenomenon is interpreted (and that is the only possible interpretation) as being a 'Ndrangheta organization.'

3. Rocco Cristello, who was murdered in Verano Brianza on 28 March 2008, had been involved in another inquiry (Operation Infinite) as a leading member of the Lombard 'Ndrangheta. He was also the subject of an operation organized by the Monza public prosecutor's office which revealed clear links with Chinese organized crime.

4. Davide Carlucci, Giuseppe Caruso, *A Milano comanda la 'ndrangheta*, Milan: Ponte alle Grazie, 2009.

5. Ibid.

6. From the 2010 report by the Italian National Council for the Economy and Labour on crime in the north it seems clear that drugs were the lever that enabled Felice Maniero to make such a big step up in the criminal underworld of northern Italy. Parliamentary commissions of inquiry and numerous

investigations by magistrates indicate that by means of drug smuggling Maniero's group became to all intents and purposes a clan. The report cites a paper drawn up by the Venice police on 7 April 2003, according to which 'the presence of drug smuggling made it possible to make a big leap forward because in the first place it put these criminals in a criminal environment that crossed regional borders and where a lot of money circulated. Another crucial element was the relationship that Felice Maniero established with some leading representatives of the criminal underworld.' A new era in the life of Brenta criminality began, because this relationship, 'as well as guaranteeing the initial supplies of heroin, also made it possible to imitate the organizational methods of those mafia groups and to adopt a more precise and structured form of association which had a characteristic hierarchy with at least a broad differentiation of roles.' The numerous crimes committed in the six ensuing years showed how far the group that formed around the figure of Maniero had penetrated.

7. The above-mentioned 2010 report by the Italian National Council for the Economy and Labour on crime in the north states as follows: 'Felice Maniero's criminal network seems never to have stopped acting on the social fabric after the boss's decision to turn state's evidence. The judicial authorities are aware of this even today. The Assize Court of Appeal in

Venice has stated clearly that Maniero's operation is a "complex of 'affairs' between people linked" to one another by a mafia-like associative bond. It "was capable, with the force of intimidation deriving from the associative relationship and the consequent state of subjection and *omertà*, of exacting behaviour that was submissive and dominated by an aberrant logic even from "extraneous individuals, victims who were forced to satisfy the criminal needs of the group". The magistrates stressed that the atmosphere that had been established was so oppressive that "the moneychangers of the Venice Casino continued to pay the Maniero gang the bribe they demanded" despite the court convictions. Neither the arrests nor the convictions were sufficient to change the attitude of people extraneous to the association. And yet this was happening in the north-west, not in some town in Sicily, Calabria or Campania.'

8. Davide Carlucci and Giuseppe Caruso, *A Milano comanda la 'ndrangheta*, Milan: Ponte alle Grazie, 2009.

9. On 23 November 2007 Modafferi and Mondella were sentenced to twenty-two years in prison for drug smuggling in the court of first instance.

10. The *pentito*'s account is indicative of the ease with which arms were moved across the borders, and the methods he

describes were not unusual. There was clearly a widespread network for supplying the criminal organizations at all levels. On 28 March 1990 the DIGOS (Divisione Investigazioni e Operazioni Speciali) of Milan and the national UCIGOS (Ufficio Centrale per le Investigazioni Generali e per le Operazioni Speciali) discovered that more than 200 machine-guns and the same number of submachine-guns had been illegally imported from Switzerland in only six months. The range of possible uses was wide – from inter-clan feuds to hold-ups of security vans and robberies from banks and post offices. The investigation, led by the public prosecutor Armando Spataro, covered Milan, Como, Verona, Pavia, Sondrio, Turin, Varese, Vicenza and Reggio Calabria. Four people were sent to prison; these included a hitherto unsuspected Milanese bank clerk, twenty-eight-year-old Vittorio Boniforti, described as 'an accountant of crimes' who kept in his home (in addition to two machine-pistols, two rifles, one pistol, 3,000 rounds of ammunition and a *carabinieri* signalling disc) a systematic account book of the movement of dozens of machine-guns. Also arrested were two young Catanians, aged twenty-seven and twenty-eight, who were captured in Geneva by the Swiss gendarmerie. The starting-point for the whole operation was the arrest of Pasquale Esposito, thirty-six, a former leader of Lotta comunista in Potenza who had later become an entrepreneur. Spataro's inquiry proved that the connection was perfectly open. The system was used by the 'Ndrangheta and other criminals to acquire weapons without having to resort to costly triangular trade agreements abroad. Further proof that the unscrupulous Swiss gun dealers were not too particular about who they did business with was provided by the case of a young Calabrian from Petilia Policastro who was charged with mafia association. He had been able to buy a machine-gun, a Winchester and a large amount of ammunition quite openly.

11. Eurispes 2008 report on organized crime.

12. Report of the parliamentary commission of inquiry into organized crime in Piedmont and the Aosta Valley, 22 July 2004.

13. Written parliamentary question and answer 4.05706 of 12 March 2003 and answer published on 26 April 2005.

Russo Spena, Deiana and Cento: 'To the Prime Minister and the Defence Minister. Given that in the locality of Isola delle Femmine in the province of Palermo there is a NATO base where munitions and arms are stockpiled, the exact nature and quantity of which are unknown; and that, since the locality of Isola delle Femmine is near the large populated centre of Palermo, it is extremely important that all appropriate precautions be taken to prevent accidents which might have a catastrophic effect on the civilian population, we wish to inquire what the nature of the arms and munitions stockpiled in that base is; whether or not that base is or has been classified as a "general NATO munitions depot"; which other bases have been given the same classification; what the nature of the arms contained in the bases denominated "general NATO munitions depot" is; whether those bases contain stores of NBC (nuclear, bacteriological and chemical) defence materials; what emergency plans have been drawn up for the civilian population of the areas surrounding those bases; what the government's intentions are with regard to the future operability of those bases; and whether in accordance with the application of the principle of caution the government does not deem it appropriate to dismantle them.'

Answer: 'First of all it should be stated that there are in Italy no munitions depots built, run and employed by NATO on the terms indicated by the document in question. Some depots currently in use do contain some structures which were built and/or extended with NATO funds – and which are therefore included in the NATO inventory – but they are in fact run by, and used for the needs of, our own armed forces. The munitions depot of the Italian Navy in the territory of the town council of Isola delle Femmine was suppressed as from 30 June 1998, in application of the dispositions contained in the ministerial decree of 20 December 1998, and the operation of removing the munitions then present in the relevant structures was completed at the end of the same year. In this connection, the mayor of the aforementioned town council, after an inspection carried out in March 2003 to verify whether or not arms were present in the area under discussion, confirmed that the base was no longer used as a munitions depot. The aforementioned depot was officially removed from the NATO inventory on 29 February 2000 and closed on 10 April of the same year, and the work of safeguarding the infrastructure through the definitive closure of the tunnels by means of structural elements was subsequently completed. Given the lack of interest in the maintenance of the facility's viability, for the institutional purposes of the Navy, the decision has been taken to decommission it. The appropriate procedure for doing this is currently being determined. In this connection, the Territorial Office of the Government of Palermo has made it known that the town council concerned has already taken steps to apply for the entire area under discussion to be entrusted to its authority so that the area can be included in the local nature reserve. As for the availability of other depots classified under the same denomination of "NATO", three such depots are currently in use; they contain naval munitions of a conventional type, and two of them contain Italian-owned material used exclusively for individual protection and for NBC testing and which therefore does not constitute any danger to the surrounding inhabited areas. Finally, with reference to emergency plans for the civilian population, the task of drawing up such plans rests with the prefectures responsible for that area, with the cooperation, where appropriate, of the Ministry of Defence. Moreover, it should be emphasized that the choice of sites for the location of depots and the security measures currently in use preclude any danger to inhabited areas.'

extracts reading groups
competitions books new
discounts extracts
competitions
books new
events books
extracts
new reading groups
interviews
events extracts books
discounts
new books events
events new
discounts extracts discounts
www.panmacmillan.com
extracts events reading groups
competitions books extracts new